Perpetuating the Family Business

Perpetuating the Family Business

50 Lessons Learned from Long-Lasting, Successful Families in Business

John L. Ward

First published 2004 by
PALGRAVE MACMILLAN
Houndmills, Basingstoke, Hampshire RG21 6XS and
175 Fifth Avenue, New York, N.Y. 10010
Companies and representatives throughout the world

PALGRAVE MACMILLAN is the global academic imprint of the Palgrave
Macmillan division of St. Martin's Press, LLC and of Palgrave Macmillan Ltd.
Macmillan® is a registered trademark in the United States, United Kingdom
and other countries. Palgrave is a registered trademark in the European
Union and other countries.

ISBN 1–4039–3397–9

This book is printed on paper suitable for recycling and made from fully
managed and sustained forest sources. Logging, pulping and manufacturing
processes are expected to conform to the environmental regulations
of the country of origin

A catalogue record for this book is available from the British Library.
A catalog record for this book is available from the Library of Congress.

10 9 8 7
13 12 11 10 09 08

Printed and bound in Great Britain by
Cromwell Press Trowbridge Wiltshire

To the many, many families who have so generously shared their experiences with me and inspired me to find the field of family business fascinating, fulfilling, and important. Thank you for what you have given me and offered to others.

Contents

List of Figures

List of Tables

Acknowledgments

This book is a reflection on more than 25 years as a student of family business. There are so many people to acknowledge and thank for what has been a most joyous career.

In the book's dedication, I thank the business families I've come to know well over many years, families who have taught me most of what I think I know. To learn while advising others is a special treat. Just as each family business is different, each has taught me something distinct.

In addition, I want to express appreciation to the students and participants in my classes and programs at IMD and Kellogg. The MBA family business students at Kellogg are the most universally uplifting, competent, and considerate group of people I have ever known. The more than 500 families that have attended the IMD "Leading the Family Business" program over the past 15 years have been pioneers in their eagerness to learn and they have served as my laboratory for nearly all of my most embryonic insights.

I also wish to thank special colleagues in the field of family business. My friends at The Family Business Consulting Group International inspire me by their genuine care for business families. Their professionalism and curiosity have taught me more than I can express. Professors Craig Aronoff, Randel Carlock, Miguel Gallo, and Ivan Lansberg are the teachers of the teachers. I am also indebted to my academic partners, Professor Lloyd Shefsky at Kellogg and Professor Joachim Schwass at IMD, for their unselfish friendship and support.

Sharon Nelton has made this book not only possible, but lots of fun. It must be rare that one finds an editor and writing partner who is not only gifted with language, but also so very versed in the subject and so very devoted to it. Pleasant and generous to work with, she has written, with heart and positiveness and insight, on the topic of family business for 20 years. Thank you, Sharon.

And loving thanks to my own family. I hope deeply that some of the lessons I have learned from other families have enhanced our lives together.

Author's Note

This is the most personal book I have ever dared to write. It grows out of years of observing long-lasting, successful, business-owning families the world over, families that have let me into their lives and thoughts and hearts. It gathers together the major lessons they have taught me about that most symbiotic of all business relationships, the family firm, in which family and business depend upon each other and work together for life, health, meaning, and, yes, even happiness.

I do not name the families that have taught me these lessons firsthand. They are or have been my consulting clients and it is my obligation to maintain their confidentiality. Where I have used them as examples to illustrate a point, I have disguised them so as to preserve their privacy. Where I have named real families and businesses, I have drawn on the public record – articles, books, newspapers, other publications, and company websites.

This is not a "how-to" book. It is not my intention to be prescriptive. These lessons are not rules that every business family must follow in order to be successful generation after generation. They are what I consider "best practices" of the most successful, long-lasting families in business. Not all of the lessons are appropriate for all families, and not all of the successful family businesses I have observed manifest all of the lessons. I hope you will pick and choose what is most right for your family and for your business.

It is my wish that the lessons on these pages will encourage you to anticipate not only the next stage of your family business but the stage after that. One of my intentions is to enable you to do for your successors what is counter-intuitive to the reality that you have faced in your own tenure as a leader and to help you feel comfortable with making decisions and taking actions that may seem to go against the grain. The lessons should also give you some tools with which to think through the "second stage effects" of the steps you are considering today – that is, the consequences that will reverberate throughout the generations that follow you.

JOHN L. WARD
Evanston, IL, USA
Lausanne, Switzerland
2004

xi

Part I

Frameworks for Family Businesses that Last

The 50 Lessons that you will encounter in the second part of this book do not stand alone. They are part of a set of broader frameworks that you will be introduced to in this section.

Chapter 1, "The Ultimate Management Challenge," describes the need for this book and sets forth the two major premises on which the book is based.

The chapter that follows, "The Five Insights and the Four P's," serves as the heart of the book, pumping blood into each of the 50 Lessons. Here is where the frameworks for the lessons can be found. Appendix B, "Integrating the Lessons," illustrates how the 50 Lessons relate to and are supported by these frameworks and should support your understanding of what goes into making a family business a long-lasting and successful one.

The idea of "stages" – or the evolution – of a family company is introduced in the first chapter and described in detail in Chapter 3, "A Vision for the Future." As you will discover, the stage of ownership a business is in shapes and defines the tasks its leaders must accomplish at a given time in order to preserve the family and the firm for future generations.

1 The Ultimate Management Challenge

Family businesses stand at a critical threshold. If you are a member of a business-owning family, you and your family's company may be very directly involved in some of the extraordinary changes that are going on in the economy and within the family business community itself. For example, look at all businesses in North America and Western Europe – large or small, public or private – and you will find that two out of five have two generations of family members working in them. For South America, South Asia, and the Middle East, the proportion of family business with two generations in them is likely to be much higher. This means that more than 40 percent of all the companies in the world are going through or anticipating a succession process – the passing of a business from an incumbent senior generation to the next generation of leadership and ownership.

Historically, however, about half of all family firms fail to make it through the next generation. Just imagine, then, the number of businesses that have the potential for being in turmoil, businesses that will underperform because of unresolved succession issues, and you will see that they make up a very substantial part of any economy. If you consider also the unhappiness and pain of the family members involved in these troubled businesses, the impact of the inability to master succession becomes a personal anguish repeated millions of times over.

A second trend poses equal potential for distress and disappointment. About 25 years ago, only 5–10 percent of all US family businesses were run and owned by teams of siblings. The rest were led, as tradition dictated, by single leaders, usually male, who had succeeded single leaders. Today, however, surveys show that 40–50 percent of the family firms in the United States will be owned and led by groups of brothers and sisters in the future. This is a change of great magnitude and it has come about very quickly. Unfortunately, we have very little experience with sibling co-owners leading family businesses as a team and consequently little understanding of how to make such teams work. Yet, a vast number of family businesses are now following this very difficult model.

As you can see, we have family businesses in great numbers undergoing two massive transformations: (1) moving from one generation to the next in leadership and ownership, and (2) adopting a still-unproven approach to leadership. What these shifts suggest is that family businesses must do a significantly better job of handling such issues as succession and leadership than they have done historically. Otherwise, as they fail or pass into hands outside the family, an enormous amount of economic resources will be wasted and the families themselves will often pay a very heavy price in terms of emotional suffering. Fortunately, we now have models of long-lasting, successful family businesses that we can turn to for guidance and help.

When I began to take an academic interest in family-owned businesses more than 25 years ago, my friends and colleagues often said, "Oh, family business. Shirtsleeves to shirtsleeves in three generations!" As a member of a business-owning family, you no doubt know the concept: The first generation creates a thriving enterprise, the second generation milks it or lives off it, and the third generation doesn't have anything left and has to start all over again.

This idea goes back centuries in time, and a similar expression is found in almost every language and culture on earth. Italians speak of going from barn stalls to the stars to the barn stalls. In England, it's "clogs to clogs (see Figure 1.1)." In Jewish cultures, it's "rags to rags." One member of a Chinese family business said to me, "Let me tell you how we say it in Chinese." The translation was, "The first generation builds a success. The second generation lives like gentlemen. The third generation has nothing left." Another Chinese expression puts it this way: "Wealth does not pass three generations."

Spanish:		
Padre Bodeguero	**Hijo Millionario**	**Nieto Pordiocero**
(Tavern Owner)	(Millionaire)	(Beggar)
Portuguese:		
Pai Rico	**Filho Nobre**	**Neto Pobre**
(Rich Farmer)	(Noble Son)	(Poor Grandson)
Italian:		
Dalle Stalle	**Alle Stelle**	**Alle Stalle**
(From Barn Stalls)	(To Stars)	(To Barn Stalls)
German:		
Erwerben	**Vererben**	**Verderben**
(Creates)	(Inherits)	(Destroys)

Figure 1.1   *There' nobbut three generations atween clog and clog (Old English)*

I found the whole idea of "shirtsleeves to shirtsleeves" a frightening one. My background was business strategic planning, a field where our whole premise is that if we do forward thinking and take certain actions today, we can shape a better future. But now I was confronted with a fatalistic concept: shirtsleeves to shirtsleeves. Was there an inevitable, natural set of laws that brought successful family businesses to their knees in the third generation? Was the concept really true or was it conventional wisdom that didn't really hold up under examination? I wanted to believe the latter, but I kept bumping into people who warned, "Oh, shirtsleeves to shirtsleeves!"

In fact, it's not just a myth. It is, unfortunately, a reality. Only about 20 percent of family businesses last beyond 60 years in the same family.[1]

Given that it's a reality, what makes it so? Why is "shirtsleeves to shirtsleeves" a phenomenon in family businesses? When I raise this question with family business audiences, they suggest these answers:

1. A company doesn't keep on top of the changing business environment. It becomes technologically obsolete, fails to recognize changing market needs, or outgrows the abilities of the incumbent management to lead it.
2. Estate and death taxes strip and defeat the business.
3. The founders' successors are often ill-prepared, unmotivated, less interested in the business than their parents, and less hungry.
4. As the family grows larger with each generation, different family members develop different interests, different values, different goals, different hopes, and different expectations. Conflicts develop and family members grow apart, sapping the business of energy, aligned goals, and commitment to continuity.
5. The environment created by one generation results in difficulties for the members of the next generation – hindering their ability to solve problems, exacerbating conflicts among them, or stifling them and making them so frustrated they leave.

When I ask these same family business audiences to choose their "favorite" reason why shirtsleeves to shirtsleeves is so frequently true, the most popular choices invariably turn out to be reasons like the last three – an ill-prepared successor generation, the fragmentation of the family as it grows larger, and the emotional environment created by the incumbent generation. The significance of these choices is that they are all *family* based, while the other two choices are more business based. However powerful the business issues may be, it is the perception of a majority of family business members that the most significant dilemmas, in terms of reaching for long-lasting success, are seated within the family. That is one of the key conclusions that I have come to as I have studied and worked with family businesses over the years and it is the first premise on which this book is based: *The most critical issues facing business-owning families are family-based issues more than they are business-based issues.* And this conclusion comes from someone, me, who has always been more business oriented.

Coming to understand this was a major turning point for me. As a business professor and a consultant, I used to argue that you've got to run a business like a business, business comes first, business is what matters, business issues are the real issues, let's focus on the business, et cetera, et cetera, et cetera. As I worked with family firms, however, I began to hear some concerns that took me by surprise. When I offered what I thought were some brilliant strategic planning ideas, business owners said, "Well now, how do these ideas fit in with our value system?" Or they asked how my suggestions would connect with the family's capabilities and the personalities in the family. Here I was, talking about marketing strategies while they were expressing concern about values and the family. Values are not something we talk about very much in strategic planning courses, and as family business owners insisted on taking values into consideration, they gave me a whole new perspective on strategy. Thanks to their wisdom, this book will show how many enduring family businesses address family issues so that business issues can be resolved.

The second major premise of this book is that *the key issues facing a business-owning family differ depending on where the business is in time, or in evolution.*

This book describes three stages of a family business: Stage I, when the founder is still in control or the successor is a controlling owner; Stage II, when a succeeding sibling generation is in charge; and Stage III, when the cousins, often in the third generation or later, have succeeded to leadership. Together, we will look at the major issues that a family faces at each juncture as well as those it confronts as it moves from one stage to the next.

What should emerge for the business-owning family is a picture – a model – of the life cycle of a family business through the generations. Because the model represents a common, predictable pattern in family businesses, a business-owning family can use it to prepare for long-lasting success instead of succumbing, through lack of knowledge, to the shirt-sleeves-to-shirtsleeves mold, becoming crippled, passing into hands outside the family, or disappearing altogether.

When I looked at the 20 percent of family businesses that had survived beyond 60 years, I uncovered a startling bit of information: two-thirds of the survivors weren't growing.[2] In the face of the commonly held belief that a business has to grow or die, how is it these non-growing companies continued to survive? One reason is that they were lucky enough to find themselves in a protected niche where customers, competitors, and technology didn't change. What I also found was that a majority of these long-lasting firms had consolidated ownership into the hands of one person, who passed it on to one person who passed it on to another single person. Sometimes the business might go from one person to two and then back again to one, through death or a buyout or some other means. But whether it was by design or by accident, what I found was that historically, ownership and leadership united in one person from generation to generation, seemed to happen most frequently.

However, the idea of finding a protected niche is no longer a realistic one. Business owners laugh when you mention it, and rightly so. Blink your eyes once and the world changes – it changes two or three times if you're in the swiftest moving industries. And while passing a business from one leader who passed it on to another seems to have worked in the past, family businesses are moving with great speed into the great experiment of team ownership and leadership.

What can family business owners do to enhance their companies' chances of enduring under these circumstances? At the core of this book are the lessons that I have learned from long-lasting, successful family businesses themselves – businesses that have made it to the third generation and beyond and that are still thriving. These are lessons I have drawn from the best of the hundreds of companies I have consulted with or studied not only in the United States and Canada but also in Hong Kong and such countries as Mexico, Venezuela, Argentina, Chile, Israel, Turkey, Bahrain, Indonesia, Italy, Spain, Portugal, France, England, Sweden, Norway, Pakistan, India, the Philippines, Thailand, Australia, and Singapore. While there may be subtle differences from country to country or culture to culture, the lessons are much the same for family businesses everywhere.

In recent years, I have been actively interviewing members of the most successful, long-lasting, healthy business-owning families that I could find throughout the world and have been trying to discover what they think they have learned. What do they think their families did right over the generations? If they could share their wisdom with other family businesses, what would they say? What I really want to know is not what went wrong, but what succeeded. The families whose lessons appear here are, in my judgment, not only successful at running businesses but they are also successful as families. Ownership has been passed on from one effective generation to another probably more than once, and today's owners in turn show promise of extending ownership and leadership to a harmonious next generation.

The lessons presented here are divided up according to the stage of business at which they *must* begin to be applied. In my view, policies, practices, structures, systems, and all the other elements that go into making an enduring, thriving business should be in place before the need. You will find, for example, that this book suggests that the founding generation develop certain policies – such as a family employment policy – not because the incumbent generation needs it but because it will be needed as the family prepares for the entry and development of the next generation and so that it will be available, in turn, to anticipate the entry of the generation after that. Likewise, the Stage II family is encouraged to start a process of "graceful pruning" to facilitate the reduction of the number of owners and avoid having ownership become discontent and unmanageable in Stage III.

Before we examine the individual stages and their accompanying issues and lessons, however, this book sets forth the five major insights and four P's, or principles, that long-lasting, successful businesses all, in my experience, seem to share. These precepts set the stage for what follows. They are the very foundation on which exemplary family businesses build and sustain their success.

Perpetuating the family business is the ultimate management challenge. I can't think of any case study you could design in a management school that would be more demanding than a situation involving passing on a family business to future generations.

What do you have to do to be successful? Two deceptively simple things. First, you must keep the business strong enough and healthy enough to last into the next generation – during an era of such rapid change that it seems like most businesses are scrambling to stay strong and healthy for just the next couple of years. Second, you must continue a healthy family into the next generation. Not only do you have to perpetuate a strong business over a long period of time, but you have to keep the family strong and solid over a long period of time as well. What's more, when either challenge would be more than enough to deal with by itself, you have manage *both* of these Herculean tasks at the same time.

These two extremely difficult endeavors are further complicated by the fact that they conflict with each other. What it takes to be successful at building a business that endures into the future and what it takes to perpetuate a healthy family are often at odds with each other. When you try to manage both processes – as you must – you quickly discover the many contradictions that are inherent when a family and a business are locked together in a unit that we call a family firm. We will examine these contradictions and how successful families manage them as this book proceeds. The dilemmas a business-owning family faces, meanwhile, are epitomized in a question I have heard over and over: "Why can't we have a family business and a happy family at the same time?"

Let me return for a moment to my field of origin, business strategic planning. As I indicated earlier, the intrinsic notion behind strategic planning is that you can take action today to shape the future. Of course, inaction shapes the future as well, but just not by design. What business-owning families do – or do not do – today will have echoes down through time, for generations to come. My fervent hope is that this book will help you become more mindful of the planning you can do and the steps you can implement that will result in the most positive outcomes for future generations of your family and your business.

This kind of far-reaching concern for the future is what has kept Seattle-based Laird Norton, a mini-conglomerate of forest-related and other businesses, thriving for nearly 150 years and six generations. The owning family's philosophy was best expressed by Nathalie Simsak, the company's president from 1988 to 1994, when she spoke of the fifth generation's commitment to serving as stewards of the company "for our children, and our children's children."[3]

By offering the lessons and experiences of some of the world's most enduring family businesses, this book aims to give you the tools you need to perpetuate a long-lasting, successful business and family of your own. It is time to loosen the grip of "shirtsleeves to shirtsleeves" and replace it with "success to success."

2 The Five Insights and The Four P's

How do they do it? How do family-owned or family-controlled companies like Marriott International Inc., Hermès, Cargill, Heineken, Nordstrom, Ferragamo, Ford Motor Company, BMW, the Washington Post Company, and many others less well known endure generation after generation? How do they become "long-lasting, successful" enterprises – businesses that are at least three generations old and that continue to be strong businesses supported by strong families?

Before we jump into the 50 Lessons, I want to begin to answer that question by sharing with you some overarching principles that many of the world's most successful and enduring business families hold in common and that guide them in blending family with enterprise. I call these "The Five Insights" and "The Four P's." Each is larger than any single lesson and encompasses many of the individual lessons under its wings. Furthermore, while the individual lessons generally fall within a particular stage of business development, the Five Insights and The Four P's transcend business stages. If a business-owning family is particularly perceptive and fortunate, it will recognize the wisdom of these principles early in the life of its business and will continue to honor them throughout succeeding generations. Other business-owning families may come to such wisdom at a later stage, and while they may wish they had recognized the value of The Five Insights and The Four P's earlier, they appreciate that these principles will stand their businesses and their families in good stead in the years to come. Think of The Five Insights and The Four P's as the framework and foundation for family business continuity. They provide the underlying shape and strength upon which the 50 Lessons – or bricks and mortar and windows and roof – depend.

THE FIVE INSIGHTS

The Five Insights are, in essence, the major keys to the enduring success of family businesses. As I observe exemplary family-owned companies, time and again I see these seminal concepts integrated into the fabric that weaves

10

family life and business operation together into a strong and beautiful whole.

Insight #1: We Respect the Challenge

Successful business families have tremendous respect for the challenge of combining family with business. They understand that the odds of passing on a business to the next generation are not in their favor. As a result of this knowledge, they take the task of managing succession very seriously and they put enormous effort into it.

One of the fundamental conclusions I've come to from my study of those who are successful at multi-generation family business continuity is that they are not "just lucky." They pay close attention to making continuity happen and they earn their success. They appreciate what is facing them and they reach out and try to learn what they can about it.

"I read every article in a major publication about family enterprises," Samuel C. Johnson told *The New York Times* the year before he retired. Johnson, the fourth-generation chief executive officer of S.C. Johnson & Son, Inc., the multi-billion-dollar, global maker of Johnson Wax and other products, said it took 30 years to create the plan that he thought would sustain the Racine, Wisconsin-based Johnson family empire. Even though he was already president and chairman, he took a sabbatical from his job in 1968, after his father suffered a stroke, to reflect on how the transition of leadership and ownership would be passed on to the fifth generation and their children.[1]

I have known many, many family business owners over the years who have taken a significant amount of time away from work to visit other family businesses and try to learn from them. If you are reading this book, you are following the same instinct. If you attend family business seminars, you are making a similar investment of time to learn from other family business owners and to develop relationships with them so that you can pick up the phone and call them when the need arises to discuss a vexing problem or gain insight into an issue.

In no way do successful business families let the challenge intimidate them. They have heard the "shirtsleeves to shirtsleeves in three generations" story, but they are inherently optimistic about their own ability to beat the odds. Members of these families say, "All our lives we've been doing things that people said weren't possible. We wouldn't be successful in business if we limited ourselves to following 'conventional wisdom.' And because we have always done things that are difficult and rare, we're a lot stronger as individuals and as a family. So we see the challenge of perpetuating a successful family business as one that strengthens us. We see it as something that makes us better. If it weren't difficult, it wouldn't be worthwhile."

In other words, long-lasting successful business families see their challenge not as an intimidating problem but as an opportunity. It's like having respect for the sea. You can drown in it or be swept away by its awesome power. Or, you can learn to swim and to navigate so that you can enjoy the water and can use it to your advantage, even sailing around the world if you wish.

Insight #2: Family Business Issues are Common and Predictable, yet Perspectives on the Same Issues will be Different

Long-lasting, successful family businesses understand two fundamental certainties: First, they recognize that nearly all family businesses share most of the same problems and issues. Second, they realize that while most of the issues they face are common to all family businesses, they also understand that different people within the same family business system – that is, a family and its business – will see the same issues in predictably different ways.

When family business began to develop as a field of study 25 or 30 years ago, consultants and university researchers like myself time and again heard family business owners say, "But my business is different! Nobody understands my problems." It took considerable persuasion and teaching and even the overcoming of distrust to enable them to see that they shared many issues in common with other family business owners.

I found that the owners of the most successful, multi-generational family businesses, however, did not need persuading. They had already discovered or intuited the fact that the issues they faced were common and predictable and that, therefore, family businesses could be studied and could learn from one another. They understood that whether your family is North, or South American, European, Asian, or African; whether it is Jewish, Protestant, Islamic, or Roman Catholic; and whether your business is in wholesaling, manufacturing, software development, retailing, hospitality, or mining, you will share most of the same issues faced by other business-owning families.

Such understanding gives a business family great power. It enables a family to realize that (a) "We're not alone," (b) "We're not strange," and (c) "We can learn from others." When a family knows that it is not alone in its concerns and is therefore not so odd after all, it gains the confidence it needs to go out in the world to secure the knowledge necessary to perpetuate its business for the long-range benefit of generations to come.

What are some of the common and predictable issues? Number One, without a doubt, is succession. In all the informal surveys I have done in my seminars, this is the issue that most captures business owners' attention. They want to know such things as: "How do I struggle with letting go?" "How do I choose a successor from among my children?" "How can I finance the transition of business ownership from myself to my children?"

How to finance business growth and family liquidity is the second greatest concern to business-owning families. Third, I find, is how to attract, retain, motivate, and reward non-family key managers. Fourth is the overall issue of compensation itself, including compensation of family members. And the fifth greatest common concern is the employment of family members – that is, who is allowed to come into the business and under what conditions? There are many other concerns, of course – such as who should be owners, how to handle in-laws, and how to educate the next generation of owners. Many of these issues will get attention in later chapters.

As a result of working with and studying hundreds of family businesses and listening to their concerns over a period of two-and-a-half decades, I have come to the theory that is the vital center of this book: *While family businesses tend to share many of the same concerns, the issues that are the most critical to any business at any point in time depend on its stage of evolution as a family business.* Is it still owned by a founder or an individual owner/manager? Is it a second-stage business owned and run by a team of siblings? Or has it evolved into a third-stage business owned by many cousins, some of whom are employed in the business while others are not? Each stage will be discussed in greater detail in subsequent chapters and you will see that the 50 Lessons are organized around the stages of ownership evolution of a business. The lessons do not specifically address the critical issues – that is, the Stage I lessons do not tell business founders how to resolve the matter of succession planning but, rather, offer practices and knowledge that have enabled successful business families to find their own way effectively through the maze of passing a business from the first generation to the second.

For now, however, back to the second dimension of Insight #2: understanding that different people in a family business will see the critical issues of family business in a different way. The wisest families understand that differences of opinion are matters of legitimate perspective, not differences of irretrievable personality. They know that if they attribute differences to personality rather than to perspective, they will slip into saying things like, "There's just no hope – you've been like that since you were three. You're acting just like you did when you were a kid." Instead, they accept that it is natural and valid to disagree, and this acceptance enables them to have empathy for one another and permits real communication to occur. It permits grown-up siblings and cousins to treat each other like adults, rather than as the children they once were.

Consider all the different perspectives in your own family business. For example, some of you will be members of the family but not hold financial ownership in the business – but you may feel an "emotional ownership" of the business because you've grown up with it and it bears your name. Some will be simultaneously both owners and managers. Some will be owners but not managers, or perhaps not even employed in the business. Some will work in the business but not be owners. Then, of course, there will be key managers who are neither family members nor owners. And some individuals who are owners, managers, and family members appreciate that not only must they balance these three roles but that they have a different perspective depending on which role they are playing at any given time.

A widely used illustration of how this works is the three-circle model of family business (Figure 2.1).[2]

The beauty of this model is that you can "map" your family on it. For instance, Ben is a family member, owner, and manager; his sister, Hannah, is a family member and owner; their cousin, Gary, is a family member but not an owner, or employee, and so on. Once you have created your map, you can develop an appreciation for how different people in the family business will see the world differently, depending on their perspective. One business owner expressed it well when he said he put on his manager's hat when he fired an underperforming and frequently tardy son; but he put on his family hat afterward and said, "I just heard you lost your job. Is there anything I can do to help?"

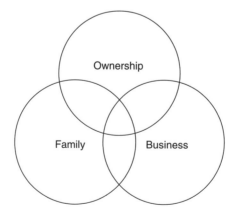

Figure 2.1   *The three-circle model of family business*
Source: Renato Tagiuri and John Davis.

It is also instructive to draw the relative size and shape of the circles 10 or 20 years hence, including the likely names in each section. That helps encourage business families to anticipate the predictable future issues they will face.

Insight #3: Communication is Indispensable

Business families with a long history of success are families that work very hard at communication. Some once-successful family companies that lost their ability to continue as family firms lay that to a lack of sufficient communication. When one firm was sold to a large conglomerate amid a great deal of family turmoil, its CEO was asked by a reporter why the family had failed to carry on with its business, "Three reasons," he answered. "Communication. Communication. Communication." What he meant, of course, was "Lack of communication. Lack of communication. Lack of communication."

Successful families recognize how profound, complicated, and perilous – and rewarding! – communication can be. The wisest dictionaries define communication as the exchange of information by many means – talk, signals, gestures, writing, or behavior. It can signify a close and sympathetic relationship or personal rapport between individuals. Good communication means that information, thought, and feelings are not only conveyed but also received and understood. It means revealing oneself and being open to others. It requires trust, vulnerability, and the willingness to raise issues that might lead to disagreement and conflict.

The way that successful business-owning families address communication is by putting in place forums or systems or structures that promote, facilitate, and assure good, ongoing sharing of information, ideas, opinions, attitudes, and feelings.

In the 1940s, Norman Smorgon created what would become the center of communication for decades to come: a big round table where family members working in the family-owned company, eventually known as Smorgon Consolidated Industries (SCI), were encouraged to talk openly and freely.

Based in Melbourne, Australia, SCI over the years engaged in enterprises ranging from meat butchering to paper production and rolling mills and became Australia's largest private industrial enterprise. According to Rod Myer, the biographer of the company's second-generation leader, Victor Smorgon, Norman fostered a "family culture of openness."[3] Norman wanted everybody to be heard and, as he saw it, a round table would create a sense of equality among family members, regardless of age or the amount of shares they held. Norman, says Myer, "believed that worthwhile ideas were just as likely to come from youngsters" as from older family members, but he knew the ideas would "only come if the environment encouraged them."[4]

As the years went on, the round table became a center for mentoring and developing the youngest generation. The teenage boys worked holidays and often joined the business straight out of school. Their lunchtimes were spent at the round table with their elders where the boys would answer questions about what was going on in their section of the business. As they developed, they were encouraged to participate in business discussions and to offer their own ideas.[5]

Even as SCI reached gigantic proportions, employing thousands, its center was still the round table, where, says Myers, "everything was discussed and decided, digested and dissected and all with something to contribute were able to speak; which businesses to go into or leave, how to expand, what to produce, who was doing well and who wasn't, how things might be improved." Family issues were addressed as well.[6]

If, based on my observations of successful family firms and on research conducted by myself and others, I could make but two recommendations to business families, both would be centered around the subject of communication:

1. Form an independent board of directors for your business.
2. Begin a regular process of family meetings.

An independent board serves as a regular forum where directors get together and talk about the future of your business. Family meetings provide a forum for communicating about the future of your family.

I have studied the link between independent boards and family business success, using a database of 7,000 family companies in research sponsored by MassMutual and Arthur Andersen in 1997 and 2000.[7] What I found was that family businesses that have independent boards grow faster. They are more likely to be international and to have succession plans. They are also more likely to have family business policies in place to guide and govern decision making. What's not known is whether independent boards cause these results or whether there is simply a correlation between these success factors and having a board. What I can tell you, however, is that having an independent board makes a fantastic difference in family business success. Doing so is the single most prevalent prescription I hear from successful, long-lasting business families.

Many business owners ask me what I mean by an independent board of directors. I have a rather rigorous definition. While such a board will have some family members and perhaps key non-family employees on it, it will also have a minimum of three independent, non-family directors who have no vested interest in the business or the family; their only interest is the welfare of both. Typically, they are respected CEOs of other companies. They are not suppliers, customers, consultants, or friends, nor are they the business's or family's bankers, attorneys, or accountants. They are truly independent, and they are available to you to help you work on the future of your business. The role of an independent board is discussed further in some of the lessons that follow – particularly Lesson #3, Voluntary Accountability.

There are two kinds of family meetings: (1) meetings where most of the attendees work in or have ownership in the business, and the business is the topic of discussion; and (2) meetings that include all family members and give them the chance to talk about the meaning of the business in their lives as well as issues other than the business. It is the second type of meeting that most concerns us here and you will find a detailed discussion under Lesson 34, Family Meetings. Suffice it to say that family meetings help family members educate themselves, pursue their hopes as a family, and come together to talk about their purpose in owning a business together.

Insight #4: Planning is Essential to Continuity

Planning in a family business is more complex than planning in any other kind of business. Nevertheless, the most successful business families tackle it willingly and intelligently. They know it is essential to their continued success.

Earlier, you saw the three-circle model of a family business. It will also be helpful to carry with you another visualization. I call it the "Continuity Planning Triangle (see Figure 2.2)."

The Continuity Planning Triangle illustrates the unique and complex challenges of planning in a family business. It demonstrates that a business-owning family has to plan on four different levels simultaneously and interdependently, producing a Business Strategy Plan, a Leadership and Ownership Succession Plan for the business, a Personal Financial Plan for family members, and – at the core of the triangle – a Family Continuity Plan.

All businesses can probably benefit from having a strategic plan – the kind of plan that answers the question, "Where are we going as a business?" In family businesses, however, the Business Strategy Plan is interdependent with the family's Leadership and Ownership Succession Plan and vice

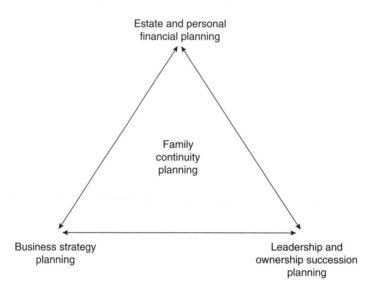

Estate and personal
financial planning

Family
continuity
planning

Business strategy
planning

Leadership and
ownership succession
planning

Figure 2.2   *Continuity Planning Triangle*

versa. In other words, your vision for the future in terms of which family members will be in the business, how many of them will there be, and what roles they will play affects your strategy, and your strategy, in turn, impacts family participation in the company.

An example: A man we'll call Jacob, the founder of an industrial chemical cleaning company and a great salesman, takes on a chemist as his partner. The partnership doesn't work out; Jacob buys out the chemist and soon takes on another chemist and makes him a partner. That doesn't work out either, and after a third unsuccessful try, he gives up on partnerships. Jacob's is for his four children – a daughter and three sons – to join him in the business, and eventually, they do. They are all talented and capable of making great contributions to the business, but Jacob begins to worry: "What if I make these four kids partners in this business? What if what happens to them is what happened to me before and we break up and the family's ruined? That is NOT what I want."

Jacob came up with a solution: he created four businesses under the umbrella of a holding company and put each of his children in charge of one of the entities. One oversaw waste-water treatment chemicals, another ran an enterprise of cleaning chemicals for food-processing plants, and so on.

In other words, Jacob designed the business around his vision for the family and the capabilities and number of children that he had. I see this all the time: consciously or subconsciously, a business strategy is designed with the capabilities of, the strengths and weaknesses of, and the number of children in mind. The number of businesses with a strategy that reflects the structure and characteristics of the family is amazing.

Is that wrong? What I have learned is that it is reality. Early in my career as an academic in strategic planning, I would have gone straight to the strategic plan without regard for the family. I would have worried that when family factors nibble into the bottom line, isn't that weakening the business competitively? I would have expressed concern that the business wasn't maximizing cash flow and profitability.

The conclusion I've come to over time, however, is that no cash-flow model I have ever built has truly reflected reality. No one can predict everything, and when something goes wrong, what you'll want is a group of people who are leading from strength, doing what they believe in, working well together, and sharing their energy and commitment to overcome disadvantages and difficulties. And when there is a fit between the family structure and the business structure, it can be very mutually reinforcing.

It is extremely difficult, however, for family business leaders to design a business strategy unless they know what the estate plan and personal financial strategy of the family are. Will the family provide money to build the business or will it conserve the money to provide liquidity for the family and pay death taxes? At the same time, it is very difficult for the family to prepare for its own security and its estate plans unless it knows what the business strategy is. There must be a link between the two. (*Strategic Planning for the Family Business* [Palgrave, 2001], by Randel S. Carlock and myself, is an entire book on synthesizing family factors and business factors into a mutually enhancing whole.)

The third linkage, often difficult to see, is between the Personal Financial Plan for family members and the Ownership and Leadership Succession Plan. I have seen many family businesses do beautiful, textbook succession planning: "The kids will go out and get this kind of experience. At this age, they'll come into the business where they'll get a wide range of coaching and experience. Several years later, they'll be managing various profit centers, and, after a period of time, they'll go through a leadership transition period working with me, the founding parent. In the fifth year of this transition, we'll transfer a third of the control to the kids, and their job descriptions will be re-defined – with the most able being named president while I become chairman of the board. Five years later, I will retire."

In reality, however, this doesn't happen until or unless the parents perceive themselves as personally financially secure. The Personal Financial Plan is interdependent with the Ownership and Succession Plan and the latter won't be executed unless the Personal Financial Plan is in place.

In the 1970s, the Smorgon family in Australia took a particularly creative and unified approach to personal financial planning. SCI doing well, but Victor, the second-generation leader, and others in the family recognized that nearly all the Smorgon capital was tied up in the business. They worried about what would happen to their wives and children in a setback. They came up with a plan: they would set aside capital from SCI and invest it in a real estate portfolio in the United States to produce income for all the family shareholders, whether or not they worked in the business. They finally realized that a family member was needed on site in the United States to oversee the family's interests. Victor, then in his mid-60s, decided to let the third generation take over the running of SCI and take on the US job himself. For the next 12 years, he and his wife spent six months of the year in New York and, on behalf of the family's personal financial security, Victor invested in more than 25 properties.[8]

Successful business families know that unless they can see all the pieces, planning cannot really take place. They understand that they must have open communication about difficult issues, that they must talk about matters that in many families would be kept secret, and that such communication requires trust and a willingness to be vulnerable. They recognize the possibility that conflict will arise over some of the issues under discussion and that disagreement can put the family at risk, but they also recognize that there is a risk to the family in *not* doing multi-dimensional planning. The family is key. I have yet to meet a business family that will risk the family for the benefit of the business. Most families tell me, however, that they are willing to do the hard work of multi-dimensional planning and are willing to take the kind of family risk associated with it as long as they see a family benefit.

The fourth plan – the Family Continuity Plan – is the glue that holds all the plans together. It is the core plan. It comprises the family's vision for itself and defines the family's mission. It answers such questions as, "What do we want to accomplish together as a family? How will we get there? How does owning a business together help us get to where we want to go as a family?" A strong and compelling commitment to preparing a future for the family makes all the rest of the pieces fall into place. It gives family members the motivation and energy to do the work as well as the purpose for which to do it.

Insight #5: Commitment is Required of Us

The fifth key to multi-generational family business success is commitment – commitment to the family's purpose, commitment to planning for the future of the family, commitment to the valuable work that takes place in family meetings, and commitment to the business and its continuity within the family.

Phil Clemens, chairman and chief executive officer of Hatfield Quality Meats, a fifth-generation family company in Hatfield, Pennsylvania, articulated commitment well when he told a magazine reporter: "It is very intentional that we want to remain a family-owned business. This is our heritage, our heirloom, something of unique value that has special meaning to our family. It is something that we protect and do not allow to deteriorate, so that succeeding generations can experience what their forefathers had birthed. We steward this asset for future generations."[9]

When Jacques Nasser was ousted as chief executive officer from Ford Motor Company in 2001 and replaced by Henry Ford's great grandson, William Clay Ford, Jr the Ford family was united behind the move. Bill Ford expressed his personal commitment to the business – and by extension, his family's – in a short speech to employees at Ford headquarters in Dearborn, Michigan. In a reference to the color of the company logo, he said, "I am both proud and determined to lead this company forward. I love this place. I bleed Ford blue."[10]

In a *New York Times* interview, he spoke of his commitment to keeping the business in the family when he called it "my children's future and my grandchildren's future."[11]

Ford family members, whose ownership of 40 percent of the voting rights in the company give them effective control of it, meet regularly three times a year. In some or all of those meetings in the difficult year of 2001, the family members had to focus on Mr. Nasser's future with the company as well as on declining sales and the crisis generated by deaths linked to Ford Explorers equipped with Firestone tires. The family's willingness to struggle through such tough issues as a group is an indication of its commitment to its historic company.

Family process itself inspires commitment. Try this in one of your own family meetings: Go around the table and ask everybody to answer the question, "What do you see to be all of the disadvantages or difficulties of perpetuating our family business?" Make a list of the answers (see Figure 2.3). Then go around the room again and ask, "What do you see to be all of the advantages or benefits of continuing the business in the family?" Again, record the answers for all to see. What I am sure you will find on the list of disadvantages is a predictable, normal list of all the classic issues that all family businesses face. This will become the core of your "curriculum" or your discussions in subsequent family meetings and will launch your family in preparing for the future.

Family members typically list the following pluses and minuses of owning a business together:

Benefits
– Opportunity to work together.
– Our mutual trust strengthens the family and the business.
– Opportunity to create wealth.
– Offers a means to pass values on to our children.
– Earns us respect in the community.
– Gives us greater influence than we would have as individuals.

Disadvantages
– Potential for personal conflict.
– Potential for disappointment when personal goals are not realized
   (e.g. getting a promotion or having one's ideas accepted).
– Too many financial eggs in one basket – the business.
– Loss of privacy resulting from greater visibility in the community.
– Vulnerability to criticism from outside the family.

Figure 2.3   *Advantages and disadvantages of owning a family business*

When you look at the list of all the advantages of owning a family business, you will most probably find yourself very inspired. Different family members will articulate different ideas about the benefits they see, but they will reflect a tremendous spirit, a tremendous vision, and a tremendous energy and hopefulness about what it is that the family can accomplish together for the future and how owning a business together can be helpful and supportive.

In my experience, families that see a rationale for continuing a business into the next generation are the ones most likely to be successful at passing the business on. They have asked the question, "How does owning a business make sense to our family?" And they have answered that question to their own satisfaction, often with such responses as, "By owning a family business together, we can be a stronger family," or, "By owning a business together, we can perpetuate a tradition of values. That is our legacy."

THE FOUR P'S

The Four P's address the fundamental dilemma of family business: what the family needs in order to be strong and healthy often conflicts with what the business needs to grow and thrive. The family needs funds to be secure; the business may need some or all of the same funds to expand. Family members must have emotional and other personal needs satisfied; meeting those needs within the business may be harmful to its success. Families and businesses are themselves a study in contrasts:

Family	Business
Emotional	Rational and objective
Basically socialistic	Basically capitalistic
Membership is permanent	Membership is voluntary and discretionary

The rules and norms of a family are different from and sometimes even the opposite of the rules and norms of a business. The business-owning family finds that the two systems collide time and time again over such issues as who gets hired and promoted, compensation of family members, valuation of the business, reinvestment in the business, and who makes the decisions. Successful business families recognize the contradictions between family and business as a given and employ The Four P's to reduce or avert the friction that these contradictions can create. Here is what The Four P's stand for.

Policies Before the Need

Wise business-owning families recognize that predictable issues are going to come up that will create some conflict or friction. They ask, "When this issue or that one arises, how are we going to deal with it?" They answer that question by establishing policies *before* the policies are actually needed. Long before the second generation is ready to come into the business, for example, the first generation develops and writes down on paper an employment policy that sets forth the requirements for family members who want to join and move up in the business. Long before there's a girlfriend or boyfriend in the younger generation's sight, the senior generation develops a policy requiring prenuptial agreements to keep the business' assets within the family. And long before the second generation enters the business, the first generation puts on paper a policy that guides decision making on compensation and performance appraisal issues.

The beauty of establishing policies before they are needed is that issues are given attention before they become personal and emotional. They can therefore be addressed more comfortably and more rationally.

A second major benefit of having policies in place before they are needed is that the business family is actually managing expectations, preparing family members for how things will work. When policies are developed and communicated effectively throughout the family, there are no surprises. Seventeen-year-old Bert knows that the employment policy requires him to complete a master's degree and get three years of successful outside work experience under his belt before he can join the family firm. He also knows there has to be a position open that can make use of his talents. Because there's a comprehensive shareholder agreement, Aunt Cora understands how many of her shares she can redeem, when she can redeem them, and under what circumstances. Because there's a retirement policy in place, Mom knows she must vacate the role of presidency when she turns 65.

If you're a member of the Raventós family, which owns, Codorníu Group, an international wine producer based in Spain, you know the requirements for becoming an executive in the company "almost from the day you're born," according to Alan Crosbie in his book, *Don't Leave It to the Children*. A good command of English is one requirement, since it is seen as the language of business. A family candidate must also have a university degree and must have worked for five years successfully at a company outside Cordoníu. Ultimately, a family council decides which family members can work in the company, and the needs of the business take precedence over the desire of the family applicant.[12] Now in its eighteenth generation, Codorníu traces its origins back to 1551.

When a business-owning family develops policies before the need, it can be much more objective than it would be if it had to make decisions in the heat of crisis. And many of the conflicts the family dreaded might not arise at all because it has managed family members' expectations.

Sense of Purpose

Enduring family businesses work very hard at defining a Sense of Purpose, the second P. They ask and discuss such questions as: Why are we doing this? Why are we working so hard? Why are we spending the time to develop policies? Why are we exerting so much energy to prepare for the future? As we learned from Insight #5, they thoroughly explore their purpose for being in business together. Families need to understand why it is that they are willing to struggle through the debates on policies, why they are willing to sacrifice so much to make the business successful, and what it is that forges their commitment to its long-term continuity. They need, in other words, to feel an over-arching purpose that makes continuing the family business worth the strife.

The Sense of Purpose will be different for each family. For one, it might be the opportunity to pass on values to future generations, to employees, and to the community. For another, it might be the opportunity to serve humanity through the products it creates.

One of the finest examples I know is that of the Ochs-Sulzberger family of The New York Times Company. For four generations, family members have come together to renew their commitment to the belief that, with their ownership of one of the world's greatest newspapers, they have been charged with a trust and an opportunity to serve humanity. As one fourth-generation family member put it, *The New York Times* was "a tradition that is far greater than any single individual."[13] As you will see below, we will get much more deeply into the Ochs-Sulzberger family as well as into a parallel newspaper family, the Binghams of Louisville, Kentucky, whose story has a far different outcome.

The loss of sense of purpose can result in the end of family ownership or in a major shift in the way a business-owning family perceives its role. The aforementioned Smorgon Consolidated Industries had its roots in bitter hardship. The Smorgons, a Jewish family, survived the Russian Revolution only to have to eke out a living in the equally hostile environment that followed. When the chance came, the family emigrated to Australia, fired by Norman Smorgon's dream of a good life built on family unity.

That sense of purpose was instilled in his son, Victor, and it guided the family and glued it together. Throughout their years of ownership of SCI and their acquisition of wealth, the Smorgons never forgot the meaning of family. Nor did they forget the family members they had had to leave behind in Russia. They retained ties as best they could and when travel to the Soviet Union became possible in the late 1960s, Victor and other Australian family members began to visit relatives whose whereabouts were known and to track down and establish contact with others.[14] Over the years, slowly at first and then more quickly as the Soviet Union crumbled, the Smorgons helped 47 Russian relatives establish new lives in Israel and Australia. Says Rod Myer: "Victor and the family offered support, making sure everyone had a home, furnishings and income for at least a year while they found their feet."[15]

Meanwhile, the family decided it was time to professionalize their business. By the late 1980s, it employed 22 family members, many from the fourth generation, and it had grown so large and complex that it had outgrown the family's hands-on style of management. With the help of the international consulting firm, McKinsey and Co., the Smorgons created a new structure for what was now a conglomerate. They brought in more outside executives and gave up much of their own managerial control.[16]

Then they found they weren't having fun anymore. The business was too much like a public company – bureaucratic and inflexible and no longer nearly as nimble as it had been under the Smorgons' more direct control. But there was no way of going back. And the Smorgons, now wealthy, no longer had the need of a family united in business to fight its way out of oppression and poverty. In 1994, Victor, then 81, and the other family elders removed themselves from the board and left it up to the next generation to decide the future of the company. Early the following year, the younger Smorgons agreed to sell SCI and a deliberate plan of divestiture was initiated.[17]

To the Smorgons' credit, the decision to end the family's ownership of its stellar company was a peaceful one. The Smorgons' respect for family and their well-honed ability to communicate enabled them to exit the business gracefully once they felt there was no longer a larger purpose to be served by continuing as the owners of SCI. This is not the end of the Smorgon story, however. We will return to them to illustrate a lesson or two, and then pick up their tale again in Chapter 7.

A compelling and inspiring purpose enables a business family to face the inherent contradictions of being in business together and gives them the energy and will to get through the inevitable tough times. It enables family members to feel they are involved in something much larger and more significant than their individual selves. More than anything else, it is what sees a family business through generation after generation.

Process

The third P is Process. A business family can never anticipate every policy it will need. The day will come when it will be surprised by an issue that is unexpected. The capacity of a family to deal with that issue effectively will be a function of its skills as a group to communicate, solve problems, reach consensus, develop win–win solutions, and collaborate. By process, I mean all the thinking and meeting and discussing that family members do together to resolve issues.

Process is what the members of the Smorgon family were engaging in every time they sat around their round table, debating the issues that concerned them and making decisions. Each shareholder had the power to veto a decision he strongly disagreed with, no matter how many shares he owned.[18] Thus, those with fewer shares had an equal voice with those who held more, an arrangement that encouraged discussion and the striving for agreement by all.

Another family business dedicated to consensus and the process that goes with it is the Salvatore Ferragamo Group, based in Florence, Italy. For more than 30 years following the 1960 death of her husband, shoe designer and company founder Salvatore Ferragamo, Wanda Ferragamo headed the company and, with the help of her six children, built it into the international luxury goods company that it is today. All the Ferragamo children are company executives (the eldest, Fiamma, passed away in 1998), and members of the third generation are beginning to take their place alongside their parents and grandmother.

According to a Harvard Business School case, the Ferragamos are known for their ability to work together and for the way they respect one another's opinions. "Wanda insisted that the family 'work as a team,' encouraging the children to iron out any differences among themselves," the authors write. "She believed the family should form a cohesive decision-making body, 'like seven arteries to the heart.' "[19]

Process is inherent in many of the 50 Lessons, and one lesson is devoted to it. When a family engages in policy making, it is bringing family members together and saying, "Let's talk about how we're going to make a decision or resolve a dilemma." The more times a family does that, the more it develops its skills of listening, communicating, collaborating, and solving problems together.

It's not so much *what* policy a family has but that it *has* a policy, which means the family members have experienced the process of developing the policy and share expectations. What I have found, for example, is that some families have liberal employment policies (any family member can join the business!) while others have restrictive rules (you can join only if you are a direct descendant of the founder, have an MBA, and have five years of outside experience). But the fact that they have a policy, they have worked on it together as a family, they have come to a consensus on it, and they have articulated it is more important than the content of the policy itself.

Parenting

One of the things that we can never underestimate is how much good parenting affects the future of a family business. After all, what is a family business about if it is not about the next generation? Yet, curiously, I have seen adults in family businesses work so hard at the business that they badly neglect parenting. This is particularly true of second-generation, sibling-owned businesses, where brothers and sisters have such big shoes to fill and work so hard to fulfill their own and their parents' expectations that they compromise time at home and time as parents.

Parents in the most successful family firms keep their attention on Parenting. Many families learn about parenting in family meeting educational sessions. They know that all the skills that are developed by engaging in Process – the capacity to communicate, the capacity to think outside of your own interests, the capacity to make decisions, the capacity to seek consensus, and the capacity to want fairness and justice for others – are the skills that you learn best growing up in your own family.

Many of the 50 Lessons go straight to the heart of parenting – lessons about communication, attitudes toward wealth, preparing for entry into the business or choosing a different career, educating children for responsible ownership, and so on. We come back to the notion of the family business as the ultimate management challenge, because when you build or run the business, you must also bring up your children, who are intimately involved in the future success of the enterprise.

A TALE OF TWO FAMILIES

After nearly 70 years of ownership by the Bingham family in Louisville, Kentucky, *The Courier-Journal* and other holdings were sold off in 1986 to new owners. The Bingham family had crashed and burned. The Ochs-Sulzberger family, however, celebrated 100 years of ownership of *The New York Times* in 1996, and the company and the family are still going strong.

Why has one of these families continued to thrive as a business-owning family while the other did not? While you will find many examples of other business families throughout these pages, we will make a closer examination of the Ochs-Sulzbergers and the Binghams.

It is only coincidental to our purpose that both families are – or were – media-owning families. What is important is that they represent business-owning families and all the joys and sorrows and successes and failures that come their way. While much has been written about both the Binghams and the Ochs-Sulzbergers, the world is fortunate to have highly perceptive, objective, and comprehensive histories of each family by a diligent husband-and-wife writing team, Susan E. Tifft and Alex S. Jones: *The Patriarch: The Rise and Fall of the Bingham Dynasty* (Summit Books, 1991) and *The Trust: The Private and Powerful Family Behind The New York Times* (Little, Brown and Company, 1999). The facts presented here are drawn largely from these two powerful accounts. I take responsibility, however, for their interpretation as it applies to family business continuity.

You will find some similarities between the two families. Both have roots in the South. Both businesses were acquired, not founded, by a family member from a hardscrabble background. Both believed in a form of primogeniture – the inheritance of business leadership by the eldest son, or, if an eldest son was not available, another son or a son-in-law.

Both families were dedicated to the crucial roles that the media, especially newspapers, play in society. For the most part, both families were liberal, but their liberalism was tempered by their Southern backgrounds.

Both families experienced untimely deaths that would have a profound impact on the business. There were, of course, some of the usual family and personal dysfunctions: alcoholism and drug abuse, divorce, envy, greed.

But there were significant differences. The Binghams were Episcopalians. They cherished the notion of going to the best schools and fought hard to be seen as the upper rung of the social ladder. The Ochs-Sulzbergers were Jews, and while they did not hide or deny that fact, the anti-Semitism they had encountered gave them reason to avoid displaying it. "We should live quietly, happily, unostentatiously," Adolph Ochs, the family patriarch, had once advised other Jews.[20]

Born in 1871, Robert Worth Bingham – a lawyer known as "Judge Bingham" for a brief period spent on the Circuit Court bench[21] – inherited $5 million from his second wife, Mary Lily Kenan Flagler, the widow of the Florida railroad magnate, Henry Flagler. It was but a small part of her $100 million fortune, but it made Judge Bingham one of the richest men in America and enabled him in 1918 to pay cash for the Louisville *Courier-Journal* and *Louisville Times*.

Bingham was a debt-ridden widower with three children when he married Mary Lily in 1916.[22] In less than a year, she died under mysterious circumstances. Rumor had it that the Judge had married Mary Lily for her money and that she had been murdered,[23] but no charges were brought against Judge Bingham. As leader of *The Courier-Journal*, his stature rose and, in the 1930s, he became Franklin D. Roosevelt's ambassador to Great Britain.[24]

Decades later, Judge Bingham's son, Barry Bingham Sr., 79 years old and the controlling owner of the family enterprises, after many years of exhausting feuds within the family, announced his decision to sell. The following day, a heartbroken Barry Bingham Jr., who had run the companies for 15 years, sadly told his co-workers that the decision represented "a failure of family."[25]

Adolph Ochs fell in love with newspapering and with the idea of bringing family members into a business at a very tender age. In the late 1860s, at age 11, he got a job as a carrier boy for the *Knoxville Chronicle*.[26] By the time he was 20, he had bought a half-interest in the faltering *Chattanooga Times* and two years later, in 1880, was able to purchase the other half.[27]

Soon after, Adolph hired his two brothers and his father. His grand plan, report Tifft and Jones, was "to provide security and employment for every member of the extended Ochs clan."[28]

In 1896, when his only surviving child, Iphigene, was four years old, Adolph managed to acquire the reputable but insolvent *New York Times*, and a legendary dynasty began to take shape.

The Bingham and Ochs-Sulzberger sagas will continue to be woven into the pages to come with the hope that their experiences will help illustrate the Five Insights, The Four P's, and, of course, the 50 Lessons. To be sure, the Binghams were not complete failures nor have the Ochs-Sulzbergers always been complete successes. They are simply human families, with a combination of wins and losses. Their stories, combined with the examples of other family businesses, can be instructive.

3 A Vision for the Future

The 50 Lessons in this book are based on my observation that there are three distinct stages in a family business (Figure 3.1). Stage I is the owner-managed era, when a business is owned and run by one person, who founded or acquired it or controls its shares. In Stage II, the business has been passed on to a partnership of siblings comprised of the two or more children of the founder or controlling owner. Stage III represents a generation of cousins who take over and then are succeeded by their children and their children's children, and so on. We call this stage a "Cousin Collaboration."[1]

Obviously, there are many possible variations in the patterns of ownership and leadership in each stage, and some of them are described below. What is important, however, is that the leader(s) in each stage be thinking about what the vision for the future of the family is and be consciously preparing for that vision. A vision for the future of the family is a manifestation of personal values. It significantly influences the plan for next-generation ownership, which, in turn, powerfully affects the choice of strategy for the business, as follows:

Family Values → Family Vision → Ownership Structure →
Business Strategy

In the last chapter, we discussed Jacob, the owner of the cleaning-chemicals company who set up four businesses, one for each child, under the umbrella of a single holding company. He did so because he feared that as partners in one business, his children might break up and ruin the family. His vision was for a unified family, with autonomous yet all-involved

Stage I Owner-Managed	Stage II Sibling Partnership	Stage III Cousin Collaboration
Ownership control is vested in one family member who leads the business.	Ownership control is shared among two or more brothers and/or sisters.	Ownership control is spread among many family members in the next or succeeding generations.

Figure 3.1 *Three-stage model of family business*

31

family. That vision, as we see, determined the ownership structure he created and ultimately shaped company strategy.

In another example, the owner-leaders of a large third-generation trading company was engaged in a strategic planning process. They were keenly frustrated in their attempts to come to consensus. "I couldn't figure out why everyone was always in disagreement," one said. "We all liked and respected each other. Then I realized how we all inherited different impressions of our founder's vision. For example, I'm convinced the founder loved the business so much he would never, ever compromise the business with family concerns. In fact, he bought out his brother-in-law when he thought he was no longer devoted to his job. My cousin, on the other hand, argues that it was Grandfather's dream to promote opportunities for his sons and for his sons' sons to work in the business and to seek their own destinies through independent, entrepreneurial opportunities that the business would provide."

STAGES OF DEVELOPMENT

Usually, but not always, family businesses are the creation of a single entrepreneur who owns or controls all the shares. Sometimes family firms are acquired and built by a single leader. In either case, this is the Owner-Managed stage of the business. As Owner-Managers age, they must decide whether to pass the business on to none or one or more children. In part, that decision is a result of practical circumstances beyond the owner's control (e.g., the number of children and their individual talents), and in part, that decision is a result of factors within the owner's discretion (e.g., who is invited into the business and the capacity of the business to accommodate family members).

If the Owner-Manager wants to keep the business in the family, it will either be passed on to another Owner-Manager as heir or be passed on to a team of sibling owners, forming a Sibling Partnership, or Stage II business. If the business is passed on to a Sibling Partnership, those family owners have a different set of decisions. They can sell the business, consolidate their ownership into one branch of the family, split the business up among the siblings, or pass on ownership to all or many of the cousins in the next generation, forming a Stage III business, the Cousin Collaboration.

There are some variations for each stage that present different motivations for ownership and/or different attitudes about leadership and governance. These variations offer a more refined list of ownership vision alternatives and, therefore, more particular implications for the business' structure and strategy.

Ownership Plans

Stage I: Owner-Managed

(a) Owner-Managed *Proprietorship*: The business is to serve the pleasure of the owner and his/her family.
(b) Owner-Managed *Capitalist*: The goal is to maximize the shareholder value of the business – even if meeting that goal results in the sale of the business.
(c) Owner-Managed *Steward*: The goal is to preserve and enhance the business for future generations.

Stage II: Sibling Partnership

(a) *Co-Managing Partners*: The siblings share equally in ownership value and power and in managerial responsibility.
(b) *Caretaker*: One sibling has ownership control, such as a trustee position or a "golden share" (one share that has all the voting power) and takes personal responsibility for the business and for the welfare of the family while all the siblings participate, usually equally, in the rewards of ownership. (As you continue to read the story of the Ochs-Sulzberger family, you will see that it closely resembles this variation in the second stage, except with respect to ownership control.)
(c) *Investment Partnership*: The siblings are all non-employed investors in the business, with a non-family executive or a non-family trustee taking responsibility for business leadership.

Stage III: Cousin Collaboration

(a) *Family Holding Company*: Some family members collectively govern the business for the welfare of the family.
(b) *Entrepreneurial Venture Fund*: Family members are encouraged to start their own ventures with the use of collective family funds. Success of any venture is usually shared, in part, with the family, and, in part, to fund future family-member ventures.
(c) *As If Public*: The business is owned and operated as if it were a publicly traded company, or it is so. Family owners can hold their shares or divest as they wish. Governance and employment decisions are made by the same standards as decisions of non-family controlled, publicly traded companies.

FAMILY ASSUMPTIONS AND OWNERSHIP PLAN

The choice to remain an Owner-Managed business or to become a Sibling Partnership or Cousin Collaboration is one of the most fundamental decisions for any business-owning family. Different families will make different decisions in large part because of different assumptions about how the family works best and how the family and business affect each other. Some families, for example, assume that owning a business together will help keep the family together. Such families may welcome a Sibling Partnership or Cousin Collaboration form of ownership.

Other families fear that sharing business ownership will bring threatening discord to the family. They might prefer keeping the family out of the business or giving unilateral control to one person. For them, remaining an Owner-Managed business or structuring a Sibling Partnership so that one family member or a non-family member has final control is more appropriate. Gekkeikan Sake Company in Kyoto, Japan, for example, has followed such a path for nearly four centuries. Founded by Jiemon Okura in 1637, it has largely been passed down from eldest son to eldest son and is now in its fourteenth generation of family ownership. For technical reasons related to Japanese inheritance taxes, the current president, Haruhiko Okura, the eldest of four brothers, owns only 5 percent of Gekkeikan. Other stock is dispersed among other entities, including a holding company, but Gekkeikan is firmly under family control.[2] Haruhiko Okura acts much as an Owner-Managed Steward, preserving and improving the business for the generations that will follow him.[3]

Early on, families develop an assumption about the relative importance of the business versus the family. For some, the preservation of the business is predominant for either moral or economic or emotional reasons. The business is perceived as the "goose that lays the golden eggs." Or the rationale is, "Without the business, the family won't have any economic support." Or, "Without the business holding us together, we will dissolve as a family." Many families feel a sense of duty to protect the business that obliges this "business first" mentality.

Those who put "family first" argue that owning a business is not worth risking family. Or they might remember the founder asserting something like, "The only reason I worked so hard and sacrificed so much time with the family is so that you could all enjoy the fruits of the business and have the right to work in the business if you wish."

Different families also have different attitudes toward leadership of the family in the future. Some cultures prefer a single leader and require that the oldest son assume the responsibility of care for all the family for all his life – often expressed as "you are your brother's keeper." Such singular leadership can be enforced with trustee power or a "golden share." Perhaps in-laws are second-class citizens. Other cultures fully empower daughters to be equal family members in all forms of membership, ownership, leadership, and wealth.

In sum, different families have different cultural assumptions and one family's may be almost the opposite of another's. Consider the following contrasting assumptions about the way families may perceive their relationship with their business.

> Business as Family Glue <–> Business as Threat to Family
>   Family First   <–>   Business First
>   Equal Empowerment <–> Single Leader

Of course, there are many other dimensions of family culture. The point is that the constellation of various family beliefs or assumptions creates a vision for the future of the family. That vision shapes the form of ownership, which then influences the character of business strategy.

BUSINESS STRATEGY

For business-owning families, strategy choice can accommodate family needs or hopes.[4] For example, a family in the lawn products business was devoted to keeping all its members as close to home as possible. Consequently, it chose to broaden its product lines and to vertically integrate, as the family grew, rather than set up operations in other, distant markets. Another family, in the media business, acquired several newspapers in different markets to give family members autonomy and to lessen risks of conflict.

Different ownership plans beg different strategies. Co-managing Sibling Partnerships often attempt to provide distinct business opportunities for each family member. Family Holding Companies and Entrepreneurial Venture Funds are designed to facilitate and coordinate the related business activities of family members. Owner-Managed Proprietorships would seem to be less growth oriented than Owner-Managed Capitalist businesses.

The following table (Table 3.1) shows some of the ways family assumptions, singly or in combination, can influence the selection of the ownership plans outlined on the previous pages and how both family assumptions and ownership plans might shape elements of the business strategy.

As members of business-owning families develop their overall family vision for their ownership plan, they should carefully consider the potential

Table 3.1 *How family assumptions shape ownership plans and business strategy*

Family assumptions	Ownership plan	Business strategy
Family first	Proprietorship	Focused, less growth oriented
Business first	Capitalist	Opportunistic, more growth oriented
Business as glue	Steward	Controlled growth, less risk
Business as glue Family first Equal empowerment	Co-Managing Partnership	Multiple business units
Family first Single leader	Caretaker	More cautious; more liquidity oriented
Business first Business as threat Equal empowerment	Investment Partnership	No distinct strategy
Family first Business as glue Single leader	Family Holding Company	Less growth oriented; likely more business units
Business first Business as glue Equal empowerment	Entrepreneurial Venture Fund	Eclectic portfolio
Business first Business as threat Equal empowerment	As if Public	No distinct strategy; perhaps less growth oriented to preserve liquidity

long-term consequences of their decisions. If they can stretch their minds to encompass contingencies, so much the better. Here are some of the questions that, depending on a family's size and structure, might be asked:

- "What if our son (or daughter) doesn't want to take over the business?"
- "What if our children don't get along – how will that affect our dream of long-term family ownership?"
- "What if our chosen successor dies prematurely or becomes disabled?"
- "How will our plans affect the third generation? What if our oldest son has five children and his younger sister has only two? Will the sister's children individually have more wealth and power than each of their cousins?"
- "What if our daughter has no interest in the business and chooses the life of a low-paid social worker? One inclination is to pass on ownership

to her brothers, who are in the business and who will take over its leadership. How would that affect the quality of life of our daughter and her children – as well as her relationship with her brothers?"

A TALE OF TWO FAMILIES (CONT.)

Understandably, many owners become exasperated by such questions. Adolph S. Ochs of The New York Times Company was one such owner. He had only one child, Iphigene, and he loved her deeply, but in his mind, a woman could not run a newspaper. Some members of the extended Ochs family hoped Iphigene would marry her cousin Julius Ochs Adler, to cement the family dynasty and provide security for generations of Ochses to come.[5] Instead, Iphigene married Arthur Hays Sulzberger, and Adolph Ochs brought both his son-in-law and his nephew, Julius, into the business.

As the years went by and the two younger men rose in rank, Adolph was torn between leaving leadership of the company in the hands of his highly respected son-in-law or those of his beloved nephew. Before he died, Adolph implied privately to Arthur that the company would be left in his care, but Adolph did not make that decision clear to anyone else.[6]

To skirt the issue, Adolph in his will created the Ochs Trust, which held the controlling shares in the company, to be distributed to his four grandchildren on the death of their mother, Iphigene. Furthermore, he named three trustees – Iphigene, Arthur, and Julius – and gave them the power to determine the next president and publisher of the company. Courageously, Iphigene took her cousin to lunch one day and told him she would be voting for Arthur – Arthur believed he was Adolph's real choice and Iphigene could not go against her husband. Besides, in her heart, she believed Arthur to be the right man.[7] "The job required flexibility and openmindedness, and Julius's attitude was often overly conservative, his approach rigid," she said in her memoir.[8] Most likely anticipating the outcome, Adolph had left Julius enough money so that he could leave the company if he so chose. Disappointed though he was, however, Julius remained in the business throughout his lifetime.

Adolph got what he had hoped for – the continuation of what had become one of the world's greatest newspapers and the perpetuation of the business in the family. But there were also unintended consequences. One was that because Iphigene lived to a very ripe old age, her children, unable to inherit, were often dependent on her for money throughout much of their adult lives.

Judge Robert Worth Bingham's choice of a successor was seemingly easier. Only the youngest of his three children, (George) Barry Bingham Sr., had joined the family business and, by the time of Judge Bingham's death, he was poised to succeed his father.

Believing that a newspaper should be in the hands of one proprietor, Judge Bingham passed controlling ownership in the family enterprises to Barry. The Judge's will also set aside a block of shares in the family companies to Mary and Barry's children.[9]

It is doubtful that either Adolph Ochs or Judge Bingham thought about what impact their decisions might have on the third and fourth generations. More likely, their chief concern was successfully passing on the business within the family upon their own deaths.

Now, however, decades later, we have more knowledge about how family businesses work. While we cannot predict the future, we can see with greater clarity how current behavior and attitudes and how actions taken now can affect families and shape business success for generations to come.

The New York Times Company provides a modified example of the model of family business ownership on which this book is based: Owner-Managed to Sibling Partnership to Cousin Collaboration. In this case, leadership succession (but not ownership) went to the son-in-law in the second generation and then to a son-in-law in the third generation before the business became a Sibling Partnership and finally evolved to Stage III.

The Bingham family business model is an example of a company that goes from a single Owner–Manager to a single Owner–Manager. Judge Bingham passed on his enterprises to a son, who in turn passed leadership on to a son. However, conflicts in the family prevented the business from continuing as a family enterprise.

Family businesses can and do succeed under either of the two basic models – single leader to single leader to single leader, or single leader to sibling partnership to cousin collaboration. For centuries, in fact, the traditional model was passing a business from son to son to son. As Gekkeikan Sake Company demonstrates, some Japanese family businesses have lasted as many as 14 generations following this path.

The choice of Ownership Plans and Business Strategy is formed by integrating many factors. Some family cultural beliefs or assumptions have been identified here; there are, of course, many others. Sometimes these family assumptions are conscious, sometimes not. Sometimes they are shared among all or most of the family; sometimes not. Frequently, the dominant force in establishing the ownership and strategic vision is the business's founder or initial family business acquirer – especially when that person is also the family patriarch or matriarch.

When the process is more unconscious and more autocratic, it's hard to separate the will or dream or vision of the founder from the ultimate decisions on ownership and strategy. Perhaps the other family members will be compliant to the founder's vision for them. Perhaps, however, there will be disharmony that will do damage to the business as well as the family.

When the process is more conscious and more participative, other factors can be considered more deliberately. In addition to family cultural assumptions or beliefs, elements such as the following can shape the ultimate choice of Ownership Plan:

- Family size. Larger families are more likely to become Sibling Partnerships or Cousin Collaborations.
- Estate tax laws. In some countries, primogeniture is tax advantaged. For many families, lack of estate liquidity shapes the feasibility of different ownership plans.
- Industry environment. Some families are able to sustain mature businesses for decades. For others, the short life cycles that result from rapid changes in technology foreclose certain options.
- Business character and profitability. The more capital-intensive a business is, for example, the less flexibility it may have to adjust for family preferences. The more profitable a business is, however, the more it can do to accommodate family choice.
- Non-business assets. The more assets the family has out of the business, the more empowering it can be to individual autonomy.

Many, many complex factors shape the choice of strategy in all businesses. For family-owned businesses, the family's assumptions and structure are key factors. Because the hopes and concerns for family are of such prominence in the thinking and decision making of many business-owning families, the choice of an ownership plan is a critical decision. Frequently, such consideration is unconscious. If the process can be more conscious, there is a greater likelihood that other factors (industry environment, estate tax laws, etc.) can be integrated into the ownership and strategic plans. When that happens, the better the business will perform and the more harmonious the family will be.

PART II

The Lessons

The 50 Lessons to follow are organized according to the three common and distinct phases of a family business that have been described in earlier chapters:

Stage I – The Owner-Managed Business
Stage II – The Sibling Partnership
Stage III – The Cousin Collaboration

Each stage has key issues and challenges that are common to that stage throughout most family-owned businesses. Those challenges are introduced at the beginning of the chapter in which a particular stage's lessons are offered. It is better to be thinking about the challenges that lie ahead as early as possible, but for the purposes of this book, the challenges are placed in the stage at which they evolve as central issues and can become obstacles to the business's future if they are not addressed.

It is important to reiterate that the lessons do not provide "solutions" for the challenges. What they do is show how successful business families position themselves to devise effective responses to the challenges that face them. This is not an answer book but a book that demonstrates what families do to create the conditions for family business continuity and success. When the right climate exists, family members are more able to join together to make the decisions and take the actions that lead to long-term family and business health.

In each of the next three chapters, the lessons are divided in two major ways:

(1) Business Perspective – lessons that are crucial from the standpoint of the business. They address issues that are critical to the life and health of the family's enterprise.

(2) Family Perspective – lessons that are essential from the standpoint of
   the family. They address matters that are fundamental to the life and
   health of the family.

As you read the lessons, you will no doubt be struck by the continuous
dance between the two perspectives – how they interact with each other,
how they often contradict each other and pose dilemmas for the family, how
one must sometimes give way to the other (and vice versa), and how, when
the family achieves the delicate balance between family and business, it
strengthens both.

While the stages of a family business are distinct, the lines between the
stages are not clear and sharp. There are periods, for example, where one
generation has not quite let go and the one to follow has not quite taken
charge. Or it may be necessary to create conditions for the next generation
of leadership that were not necessary to the current leadership.

During these transitions, long-lasting family businesses find it works to
have the lessons of the next stage in place before the next generation takes
over; therefore, it becomes the responsibility of the current generation to
give them thought and set them in motion.

Remember back in Chapter 1 when we talked about the reasons family
business owners gave for the failure of a family business to thrive? Most of
the reasons they offered were rooted in the family – ill-prepared family
successors and so on. Perhaps it shouldn't be surprising, then, that a
substantial majority of the lessons – 31 of the 50, in fact – are Family
Perspective Lessons.

4 Stage I: The Owner-Managed Business

Initially in a family business, ownership control usually resides with one person, the founding entrepreneur – or, as in the cases of both the Bingham and Ochs-Sulzberger families, with an individual who acquired the business. This is Stage I, the era of the dominant Owner-Manager. While the Owner-Manager may distribute some shares to others – for estate planning purposes, for example, or to obtain growth capital – he or she typically retains voting control and leads the business. Now and then, control in the first stage of a business may reside with two or more founding partners, but for the sake of simplicity and because single-ownership is far more typical at this stage, we will limit our observations to the single Owner-Manager.

In a very real sense, the Owner-Manager is king (or queen!). The business centers around him and depends on him, and the family most likely does, too. His achievement in founding and/or building the enterprise lends him a hero's status, gaining him respect and admiration in the community. The business is a reflection of his vision, his persistence, and his courage. It is his creation, his life's work, one that has brought him both wealth and stature. Who would want to give that up?

Most Owner-Managers don't. The most critical issue of a first-stage, Owner-Managed family business, from a *family* perspective, is the issue of the entrepreneur's letting go of control. From a *business* perspective, the most pivotal issue is the availability of a qualified successor. Is there a competent heir, someone in the next generation who is willing and able to take over the leadership of the business? Someone who can follow in the footsteps of a powerful hero?

When I was a professor at Loyola University Chicago, we conducted a two-year study on the issue of letting go of control via a focus group made up of 10 owners, all over 65, who all said, "I can't do it." What we found was that, to them, letting go of control of their businesses meant losing their identity. "What would I do?" they asked. "What would I tell people at the country club what I do for a living if I don't have this? This is all I know. This is what I do." They told stories of friends or relatives who retired and whose lives ended. Some, they said, died of a "broken heart."

43

The spouse conspires in the entrepreneur's resistance to retirement, too. Audiences titter when I repeat the old saw, "I married you for better, I married you for worse, but I didn't marry you for lunch." They know the last thing a wife wants is a hyperactive, Type A personality with a high need for control suddenly at home, telling her how to run a household that she has capably managed for 30 or 40 years.

Frequently feeding the entrepreneurs' fear of retirement, the study showed, was a deep-seated concern about financial security. "If I let go of control of the business," they worried, "who will make sure that my spouse and I will live out the rest of our lives never in want of money?" They felt that if they retained control of the business, they would have access to the resources that would assure their financial security.

What we found, however, was that the financial security issue was far more one of perception than of reality. In most cases, these entrepreneurs were set for life. Their view of their position, however, was reminiscent of that amusing statement attributed to John D. Rockefeller Sr.: "You know what financial security is? Financial security is one more zero than you have." If Rockefeller didn't feel financially secure, who could?

Underlying the concerns about loss of identity and financial security, however, was what we believed to be the entrepreneurs' real issue in their inability to let go: *control of the family*. They believed that as long as they had control of the business, they had control of the family. Curiously, they felt that love and trust were not enough. They believed that control of the business would give them access to the family. "If I didn't have control of the business, I'm not so sure I'd see my grandkids as much," was a frequent comment.

Over time, through professional coaching and coaching one another, the entrepreneurs in our study came to replace their negative images of retirement with positive ones. They came to understand that there was life after leaving the business – they could teach, write, or start another business. They became more realistic about their financial security, either recognizing that they had it or taking the planning steps to achieve it. They also began to look at the notion that their position in the family could be separated from their control of the business.

For the succeeding generation in a family business, the chief frustration is coping with an entrepreneurial parent who can't let go. For the parents, however, the issue is how to select among their children for business ownership, control, and leadership. Non-family employees see the key concern as the qualification and competence of the successor. But none of these issues is relevant if there's no successor at all. Surveys show that nearly one-third of all Owner-Managers over the age of 60 have no available successor in mind.

As indicated earlier, family businesses are characterized by contradictions. Even when the succession goal is merely to pass a successful entrepreneurial business on to a single heir, there is a tricky contradiction. The more successful the founder, the more complicated it is to attract a very competent successor. The successful entrepreneur can be quite a legendary figure, chasing away many who don't want to follow in his footsteps. Often it seems as if those chased away by the shadow of a great predecessor are the most entrepreneurial offspring. They want to carve out their own niche. They have been conditioned by their parent to believe that starting a business is a more noble calling than inheriting one. Yet, for the entrepreneurial business to go on to the next generation, competent heirs must be attracted.

The entrepreneurs who are most successful in drawing competent heirs into the business are those who see their role as stewards. That spirit of stewardship makes them more selfless so that they are less intimidating heroes. It also makes them more eager to do what it takes to attract excellent successors – including going against their own nature or perceived self-interest.

Controlling Owner-Managers are often marked by a belief in individualism, a need for personal control, and a desire for secrecy and privacy. When the Owner-Manager makes critical decisions, the emphasis is often on his own personal priorities. These characteristics, of course, will influence the upbringing and orientation of the successor generation. While these traits can often be suitable for a first-stage business, especially a smaller one, they can be counterproductive to the long-term effectiveness of the second-stage generation, the siblings.

Leaders in the second stage, the Sibling Partnership, need to be an excellent team, collaborating with one another and resolving conflicts together – just the opposite of their Owner-Manager parent's inclination toward individualism and personal control. This contradiction is often evidenced around the dinner table or on a family car ride. If a conflict arises among the young siblings, the entrepreneurial parent will often autocratically and promptly resolve it, depriving the next generation of the opportunity of learning how to struggle through the conflict–resolution process among themselves. The more successful the venture is and the more consuming and exhausting the CEO's job, the more forceful the entrepreneurial parent is likely to be – and the more commanding at home.

The most effective sibling partnerships I have seen come from families that are not dominated by an autocratic, take-charge entrepreneur. Sometimes the business predecessor to the siblings wasn't an entrepreneur at all but was, perhaps, a non-family executive filling a leadership gap after the early death of a parent-entrepreneur, or a parent who was an inheritor. Most often, successful sibling partnerships seem to come from families where the non-business parent (usually "Mom") clearly controls the next generation's upbringing and does so with a culture that is powerfully supportive of teamwork. When successful sibling partnerships evolve, they emerge from environments in which parents don't follow the typical decision-making style that puts an emphasis on the entrepreneur's personal priorities. Instead, they create a decision-making style that puts family first.

With that as background, let's move on to the Stage I lessons.

LESSONS LEARNED

Essential from a Business Perspective

Lesson 1   Social Entrepreneurs

The pace of business is so fast today that a new kind of leader is needed for family firms. Typically, a family business CEO leads a company for 20 or 30 years or more. In the most common pattern, an entrepreneur, often after much trial and error, hits upon an idea that clicks with a market opportunity. She builds that idea into a success, and runs with that success until it peaks out. The business then goes into a long period of stagnation. If the business is lucky, the next-generation leader comes along and creates a success all over again. In other words, the classic pattern of the family business that is able to grow from generation to generation is that each leader creates and grows one strategic success, and then it stagnates; the next-generation leader comes along and does the same thing. Each generation, then, brings about its own strategic renewal.

However, this pattern no longer represents a viable model. A family business cannot endure in an environment where competition is changing and intensifying at a tremendous pace unless it is led in a way that it can renew its strategy more often than it changes leaders. The head of a family business today must be able to lead an organization through two or three or four waves of strategic renewal during the 20-year or 30-year period that she is in charge. Such leaders are very rare. Wondering what characterizes people who can build multiple waves of strategic renewal in an organization, I sought such leaders out. I call them "social entrepreneurs" because that's how several of them, in our conversations, referred to themselves.

In my observation, social entrepreneurs share the following four traits:

(1) *They have an "incompletable mission."* While they may have goals like growing the business 10 percent per year or increasing shareholder value from $40 to $60 a share, they are not motivated by such goals. They

are driven by missions that force them to reach out into the future and to seek continuous improvement.

They will never be self-satisfied because their mission can never be achieved. A typical mission of such leaders is *to build an enduring institution*, one that has the capacity to sustain itself and to maintain its excellence after the leader is gone.

(2) *They believe they are the creators and developers of a philosophy of management.* They are not as eager to talk about their products or their customers as they are to discuss their theories of management. They take personal responsibility for what goes wrong in the business. If there's bickering between two departments, the social entrepreneur thinks, "Obviously, my management model is not yet perfect. What can I do to improve it so that this kind of conflict won't happen again?" Their goal is to create an organization that can manage itself and perpetuate itself.

Social entrepreneurs believe so strongly in their philosophy of management that they are convinced that other institutions could benefit from it, and they are very willing to share it – with the local school system, for example, or a non-profit organization.

(3) *They are active in the world of ideas.* Social entrepreneurs have the courage to be role models. They are eager to take their philosophy of management outside their organization to test it and get feedback on it as a means of engaging in continuous improvement. They are people who are willing to go to universities and say, "Let me tell you how I think I manage. What do you think?" They talk to their trade associations about their theory of management, and they open up their companies to visitors, telling them, "This is how we do it."

A number of them even write books to get their ideas across. One such entrepreneur was the late Dave Longaberger of The Longaberger Company, a billion-dollar Newark, Ohio conglomerate best known for the baskets it manufactures and now in the hands of its founder's two daughters, Tami and Rachel. In his book, *Longaberger: An American Success Story*, he not only tells stories about his vision for the company and his loving grooming of his children for leadership, but he also shares his philosophy of leadership in a chapter called, "Eighteen Management Principles That I Live By." Afflicted by stuttering and epilepsy as a child, Longaberger didn't graduate from high school until he was 21 and he elected not to go to college. But, as his achievements prove, that didn't mean he wasn't smart. He wanted to share with the rest of the world what he had learned about leadership and, a year after he was diagnosed with cancer in 1997, he began work on his book project with writer Robert Shook.[1] Longaberger passed away in 1999 and the book was published posthumously.

(4) *Social entrepreneurs see themselves as stewards of the business.* Even though they may have absolute control of the enterprise, they are not possessive about it. It's not "my" business. They depersonalize themselves from the business a little bit and regard it as an institution worth preserving in its own right. As Tami Longaberger, now CEO of the family business, observes in the foreword to her father's book, Dave Longaberger was always looking ahead. "In our meetings Dad would say, 'In a hundred years, we'll all be dead, but what will the company look like? What will it be trying to accomplish?' .... He wanted these questions to be the guiding spirit at Longaberger."[2]

The social entrepreneur's four characteristics all intertwine. If I see myself as a steward, I'll want to preserve and enhance the business. To do that, I need a philosophy of management that allows people to grow and develop so they can take over the institution and so that it can endure without me.

This combination of characteristics is fully consistent with a leader who can run an organization that is able to constantly renew itself strategically over time. If it can't renew and grow, the business may never be large enough, healthy enough, or elegant enough to attract and support a growing family throughout many generations.

Furthermore, being a social entrepreneur helps the Owner-Manager address the two critical issues facing a family business in Stage I – the question of whether there is a competent successor and the ability of the founder to let go. By definition, the social entrepreneur is committing herself to letting go, since her mission is to create an institution that can sustain itself beyond her own leadership and life. As part of the process of creating a management philosophy, the social entrepreneur will develop leadership in the next generation to take over – probably in the form of a son, a daughter, or a team of siblings.

The business also benefits in other ways when its founder is a social entrepreneur. The example of business growth has been set from the beginning, which means the business's expansion is accelerated beyond what it otherwise might be. Most likely the founder has also set a goal that the business must achieve by the second generation – that of making the business attractive to the most competent young family members.

Lesson 2   Irrevocable Retirement

Successful family businesses have learned that having a fixed retirement age that is evenhandedly applied to everyone in the company, especially to the family, is very constructive. Very few family businesses figure this out in the first stage, but because they struggle with it in the first generation or perhaps the second one, they eventually come to recognize the value of an irrevocable retirement date. This amounts to a mandatory retirement policy, which might be, "You'll retire from the family business at 65." Or, "You must retire from the board at 70."

While a mandatory retirement date addresses the delicate issue of the leader letting go, it does much more than that. The value of a mandatory retirement policy is that it creates the opportunity for more changes in leadership in the later stages of the business. In the third or fourth generation, for example, you may have brothers and sisters and cousins who are six or 10 or 14 years apart in age. Very often in older, successful family firms, you'll see two or perhaps even three CEOs from the same generation. A first-born child retires from the top position at age 65, giving her 57-year-old brother an eight-year run as CEO. When a younger member of a sibling partnership knows that there's still an opportunity for him to be CEO after an older brother or sister retires, that helps motivate him and also helps hold the sibling partnership together.

A mandatory retirement age also creates growth opportunities for other people in the organization, family members or not. If you have two brothers and a sister slotted into a company's only three vice presidencies and they hold those positions until they die, there's very little opportunity for growth for non-family employees who might aspire to senior-level leadership. But when you have a mandatory retirement policy, you make your company more attractive to good non-family people because they see some opportunity for themselves.

A set retirement age also catalyzes the succession planning process in a family business. If a CEO can retire at his own wish, he may never get around to retiring nor to addressing the matter of a successor. But when a 60-year-old CEO knows he must leave the company in five years, he starts to think, "What's coming next? How do we prepare people for leadership? How do we evaluate them? How do we test them? How do we present them to our board?"

When there isn't a mandatory retirement policy and the leader is doing a succession plan, it's important that he attach a retirement date to it and announce it to the whole organization. He might say, "I want to prepare you to become the next leader, and I will transfer control and authority to you on January 1, 2010." By announcing his decision to the organization – or, at the very least, to an independent board of directors – the incumbent CEO is making himself publicly accountable for implementing his plans and is much more likely to live up to his commitments.

When the CEO doesn't attach a retirement date to his succession plan, he may be tempted to adopt a perpetually rolling five-year plan. At 60, he tells his son, "In five years, I'll turn the business over to you." Then at 65, he says, "I'll turn it over to you when I'm 70." When he's 70, he says, "Well, we didn't achieve all we needed to achieve. I'm going to stick around another five years."

There's no magic retirement age. What's important is the finality of the decision, and its clarity. Some successful family businesses lean toward an earlier age, such as 62 or 65, because, again, letting go creates more opportunities sooner for organizational and leadership renewal.

One final thought about that critical date: Ownership control should also be transferred by a set time. There are three things that the senior generation passes on to the next generation – responsibility, authority, and ownership control. If you, as the incumbent CEO, pass on only the responsibility, you are essentially saying, "I'll be the CEO, but you do the job." If you pass on authority, you're saying, "You're the CEO. You do the job. But I really am in control and I can change my mind or influence you any time I want to." No succession is complete until ownership control has transferred to the successor generation.

Lesson 3   Voluntary Accountability

Some of the finest family business leaders I've met take the attitude that "I know I'm better if I'm accountable," and they volunteer to be accountable in a number of ways. One way is to put in place a truly independent board of directors and to take it seriously. Such a board would include highly qualified outsiders, such as other CEOs, that the family business leader is willing to share sensitive information with and listen to. What makes this "voluntary" is that the family business leader doesn't have to do this.

In 1998, after creating a board of directors that included knowledgeable outsiders, the fifth-generation leaders of Al. Neyer, Inc., a Cincinnati Ohio, commercial real estate developer, explained their decision in the company's annual report: "By putting outsiders in this influential position, the accountability of the management team has been raised and a more professional standard has been established."[3]

While there are many legitimate reasons for having a board – it is a wonderful resource for strategic planning, it can help you resolve conflict and choose successors, and so on – the kind of leader we're talking about is one whose main reason for having a board is to have someone to be responsible to. You don't often find leaders who are willing and able and courageous enough to volunteer for that kind of accountability.

There are other forms of voluntary accountability. I find really successful family businesses to be very willing to share financial results and performance with others – both inside and outside the company. Even though they are 100 percent privately held, some of the most successful family companies – Al. Neyer, Inc., among them – put together an annual report as if they were public and send it to their suppliers, their customers, their bank, and individuals within the company, as well as family shareholders. "These people have a right to know how we're doing. They depend on us," is the belief of these companies. "Would you rather do business with a company that says, 'I don't want to tell you what I'm doing?' Or would you rather do business with a company that's forthright?"

Companies that disclose information so openly believe doing so gives them a great competitive advantage. It's not hard for them to do because they just cannot imagine a different path. They believe they are an institution in a society to which they have responsibilities.

A family business leader's commitment to being voluntarily accountable sets an example of responsible ownership for future generations of owners. When it's the Stage I CEO who makes this choice, the precedent is already established by the time the Stage II successors take up responsibility for the business. By the time the business reaches the third stage, family members who may each own only 7 percent of the company and who do not even work in it will have inherited a tradition that says, "As an owner, I have a certain accountability. I owe something to the company and something to society."

Not all companies will want to go all the way when it comes to disclosure. Going totally public with financial statements may not be the right thing for every business. But a mentality that fosters accountability, whatever form it takes, is one that characterizes successful, long-lasting businesses.

Lesson 4   Principle of Merit

From the outset, a family business needs to operate on the principle of merit. Putting policies in place that focus on competence and earned privilege and discourage paternalism is just a sound way of conducting a business. Merit plays a role in many areas of a company, including determining who is qualified for employment or promotion, how people are paid, how a successor will be selected, who will serve on the board, titles and responsibilities, and incentives.

Just as important, the family needs to adopt and support merit as a value not only for the business but for the family itself. Successful business families have found that the earlier a family makes merit a part of its value system, the better – before the concept has to be tested in an awkward or uncomfortable situation. Otherwise, a business owner might be tempted to hire a brother not because he's competent but because he's out of work, or a family member might be invited to serve on the board not because she has something to contribute but because her feelings might be hurt if she's not asked.

Although we've identified the principle of merit as a Business Perspective lesson, it offers one of the clearest illustrations of a situation where the family's interests and the business's interests intersect. At first it might appear that conducting the business on the basis of merit contradicts the interests of the family. After all, if you operate on merit, you won't hire that brother or put your aunt on the board without sound reasons. You won't promote your daughter, either, if she's not ready. But in fact, operating the business on merit works in the best interest of the family as well as the business. Caring business families don't want to put their children into positions where they don't know whether they've really earned their way. Caring parents say, "We want people to feel that what they have achieved is truly the result of their own contribution and effort, and not something given to them because of their name or because they are the boss' son or daughter."

If a family is not clear about the value of merit, a son might take the fact that he was passed over for a promotion as a sign his parents do not love him. But when merit is the operating principle in both family and business, parents can say, "Because we love you, we feel it's important that you earn your privilege. Otherwise, you're not going to know who you are. You're not going to feel good about yourself or have the self-esteem that you deserve."

Codorníu, the Spanish wine-making company, was demonstrating the principle of merit with its family employment policy, described in Chapter 2. When the principle of merit is inculcated as a value while children are very young, they become conditioned to believing that operating on merit is the best practice. They also understand clearly what is expected of them if they wish to join and rise in the business.

Lesson 5   Attract Most Competent Family Members

One of the most difficult questions a family business faces is: how do you attract the best people in the next generation into the business to become its future leaders? It's a particularly prickly question when you are going from Stage I to Stage II – competent young family members know that they have opportunities elsewhere and may not want to live in the shadow of a heroic Stage I leader. They may also know that Mom or Dad is the kind of person who will be reluctant to let go and that it may be a long wait before the next generation can take over.

If the family does not embrace the Principle of Merit, the family members most likely to come into the family firm are the ones who are least competent in business, while the most competent family members will look for challenging opportunities elsewhere. The most competent family members have options, and they will want to go where their achievements are recognized. They see that the family business is not run in a professional way, and they don't want the burden of carrying incompetent family members and trying to make the business successful in spite of them. The sad result is that the business loses the very people it needs to keep it healthy and thriving.

To achieve the goal of becoming a long-lasting, successful business, you have to give thought to how you are going to make your business attractive to the most promising next-generation family members. What would it take to make them see the family business as an interesting career opportunity? Again, you have to begin taking action when those family members are quite young.

Many families start their children with after-school and summer jobs. Very likely, they're given menial work – a lawn-maintenance job or a job on the shop floor – so that they have to prove they can do what entry-level employees do. It's good for them to get that basic experience, but what will ignite their enthusiasm about the company is to give them a special project as well – such as conducting some simple research or drafting a report. Or you could take your son or daughter on a trip to visit a customer or a competitor, or to attend a trade show.

Many parents insist that their children start at the bottom and work their way up in the company. That's fine, as long as the parents aren't obsessive about it. Young family members should have the opportunity to learn what it's like to do the tough work of hourly employees. At the same time, you want to give exciting and attractive opportunities to sons and daughters who have the greatest enthusiasm about the business and show the greatest promise.

As children become young adults, compensation takes on increasing importance and must be thought through. A son who's a newly minted MBA will be resentful if you insist that he has to start at the bottom ("Because that's the way things work around here and there are no exceptions!") and be paid £22,000 a year when he could go to another company and earn £50,000 to £60,000. Maybe there's a way to compromise. If your son took that high-paid job, he would probably be working 60 hours a week. Suggest that you'll pay him an annual salary of £22,000 for 40 hours a week, and then offer him a bonus of £30,000 for working an extra 20 hours a week on a special project – such as doing industry analyses or coming up with solutions for knotty computer problems.

Culture, however, often shapes such decisions. Y.B.A. Kanoo Group, a sixth-generation family business based in Manama, Bahrain, is a conglomerate with businesses ranging from shipping and travel to commercial trading and insurance. In *The House of Kanoo*, his history of the company, Khalid M. Kanoo, an executive in the company, points out that usually "the salaries of the married male members of the family are the same and several houses are built at one time to house those of a similar age." The houses, too, are similar and occupy about the same amount of land. The arrangement, he says, is not uncommon in the Arab world.[4]

Some family business cultures also have a tradition of welcoming all family members who want jobs. Smorgon Consolidated Industries had "a place for everyone," including sons-in-law, according to Myer. But the Smorgons also had a unique ability for making use of people's different talents, and family members were not promoted beyond their ability to succeed.[5] Norman Smorgon, the first-generation leader, admired one son-in-law, Joe, for his acumen with numbers and markets, and another, Mossy, for his character and work ethic. Norman would say that "one of my sons-in-law is a gifted businessman and the other is a gifted husband."[6] The implication was that Mossy would not make it to a top job in the Smorgon business, but nevertheless, he was loved and valued by the family.

It takes creativity to make a business alluring to talented sons and daughters. As you consider what's appropriate for your family and your business, think about how your employment and parenting and management philosophies and the way you approach young family members all affect the ones you most want to come into the business.

Again, the concept of the "social entrepreneur" is a useful one here. Social entrepreneurs not only create the economic engine for continued growth but also the philosophy of management that is exciting to the most business-competent young family members. They are also committed to preparing new leaders to take over and to entrusting the business, at the appropriate time, to new hands.

Lesson 6   Many Non-Family Executives

A family firm not only needs competent family members in the business but also a cadre of strong, non-family managers who can bring fresh thinking, challenge, and a diversity of style and perspective to the organization. Smart business families, therefore, spend ample time thinking about how they can create opportunities and space for talented outsiders.

In the 1920s, Cargill, Incorporated initiated a policy of aggressively recruiting potential managers right out of college and training them for greater responsibility. The policy would stand the Minneapolis-based company in good stead three decades later when three family members in top management roles died in rapid succession. The younger family members were not yet ready for major roles, but fortunately, the company had three talented non-family executives it could turn to. All had been brought into Cargill when they graduated from college and had risen through the ranks. They were as effective as the family management team they had had to replace, and Cargill's policy of hiring and developing non-family talent is seen as a key to its success.[7] Once known as a grain company, Cargill, now a diversified international conglomerate with 97,000 employees, is recognized as the largest privately held company in the world.

Some families establish guidelines. "We don't want more than one-third of the top jobs in the business held by family members," say the owners of one family firm. They know that if they have a lot of family members working in the company, they have to really build it because they have to save room for the two-thirds who are not family.

Another approach that some successful business families take is to stipulate that there will be more divisions or departments in the company than there are family members to fill them. "We want to have opportunities for non-family people to run profit centers for our company," they reason. "We want them to believe that there's a good career for them here and that there's an opportunity for them to achieve a very high level of responsibility." Such families want their excellent non-family people to know that they can aspire to the highest ranks of the organization and that they don't need to fear being choked out because of an overabundance of family members.

The most successful Owner-Managers believe you need to look at how many family members are already moving up the executive ladder or are expected to come into the business and how many non-family executives it is desirable to have. Then you need to do two things simultaneously: structure your business to make sure you have room for both groups, and design your family employment policies so that you can accommodate both. Suppose yours is a smaller company and you have a large family. You sense that there are a lot of family members who would be interested in joining the business. In order to save room for talented outsiders, you may have to develop an employment policy that raises the bar even higher for family members and permits only the best of the best to join the company.

Some companies go a step farther and look at how they can create room not only for non-family executives that are groomed from within but also for excellent, proven, non-family executives to come into the organization later in life. One company's policy provides that one-third of the top jobs can be held by family, one-third are to be held by non-family people who have been promoted through the years from within, and one-third are to be filled by experienced non-family executives who have been hired within the last three to five years.

As of the year 2000, Codorníu had 144 family shareholders, of which only seven worked in the business. Codorníu tries to keep family members limited to about 1 percent of its total employees and to make room for talented non-family executives to rise to the highest levels.[8]

Whatever the approach, successful business families find that bringing in seasoned non-family executives is an excellent way for a family company to gain both wisdom and outside perspective.

Lesson 7   Opportunities for Wealth

To attract excellent non-family executives, a family business not only has to provide them with good career paths, but it must also compensate them adequately and competitively. Family businesses have to vie with the marketplace for the services of the very best non-family executives. In other situations, particularly large companies, excellent executives have opportunities to create personal wealth through stock options or equity incentive plans. Family businesses, to be successful at recruiting and retaining excellent outside executive talent, must also provide opportunities for creating wealth. This means more than paying non-family executives well – there's a distinction here between a good income and wealth. Wealth means having a sizable nest egg – on the order of a million euros or more – at the end of one's career.

Generally, family businesses do not want to distribute shares of the company to individuals outside of the family because they do not want to dilute family ownership and control. However, they find other ways to enrich their most valuable executives. Some owners offer a "pot of gold" to an executive who stays with the company for a designated period – for example, a €1 million bonus after 10 years or a lifetime annuity for an executive who stays until age 62.[9]

Other business owners offer long-term bonuses linked to company performance or phantom stock, which acts like real stock without conferring rights of ownership. Still others give top non-family executives equity in another of the business-owning family's investments, such as real estate, or in a side venture.

Whatever option is chosen, it should provide for the security of the prized non-family executives, and it should say, "We appreciate you for all that you've done – and are still doing – for our family."

Essential from a Family Perspective

Lesson 8   Family First Environment

In the Owner-Manager stage of a family firm, whether you've acquired the enterprise or started it, the business is the center of the universe. Everybody in the family puts the business first because its survival is at stake. Dad doesn't get home from the business until 23:00 hours, and then he's tired and grumpy. But his wife and kids say, "That's okay, Dad. We know you love us." Mom does the company bookkeeping at the kitchen table. After school, the kids move boxes, sweep the floors, and work the cash registers. When the family is lucky enough to have dinner together, what do Mom and Dad talk about? The business!

The problem with being business-centric in Stage I is that it creates a long-term mentality that says the only way you can be close to the family is to be in the business. If anything matters to you more than the company, you're seen as not committed or as betraying the family. For the children, it means, "If I don't join the business, I'm being disloyal to the family. If we want to be together as a family, we've got to be in the business together."

When a family makes the business its central priority, its identity as a family becomes enmeshed with that of the business. The notion that the business is more important than anything else gets carried into the future.

The lesson that I've learned from successful family firms is that as soon as possible, the family needs to understand that the family is more important than the business. This doesn't mean compromising the business or not working day and night to assure its survival. What it does mean is recognizing that the business is not the family; the family is the family. Codorníu offers an example. In 1983, disagreeing with the way the company was going, one branch of the family sold its shares back to the business and started its own winery. The current president, Maria del Mar Raventós, experienced some criticism because she maintained friendly relations with the dissident branch. However, she has known its members all her life, and played with some of them as a child. "I think it's a nice thing – to be able to make the distinction between what is the job or what is the company and what is the family," she said. "They are quite different things."[10]

In the most successful family businesses, even when the business is an incredibly intense, consuming endeavor, the parents find a way to disconnect from it. When they're with the family, they focus on the family. They recognize that the family is important in its own right. They know family members can share interests other than the business and enjoy one another and just plain have fun together because they're a family, apart from the business.

The sooner a "family first" environment is established, the better. It's especially difficult to do in Stage I because the business gobbles up the family's time, identity, and energy. But even under those circumstances, most enduring business-owning families have been able to make time for family, time when business is off limits.

When business always takes precedence, it's not unusual to find conflict between generations and conflict within the next generation. Sons and daughters who join the business may resist working the long hours their parents have put in. The parents may view them as lazy, while the children may declare, "I want a balanced life."

Fragmentation of the next generation occurs when some of the kids seek to please their parents by accepting the business-centric model and trying to be responsible and conscientious, while their siblings reject that model because they find it so oppressive. A business-first orientation can also be a painful source of conflict for sibling partnerships, when one sibling emulates the parent's model and another wants to enjoy a more balanced life without being perceived as not being committed to the business. Whatever the parent generation can do to nurture a "family first" environment will help to avoid this kind of backlash and divisiveness. At the very least, consider setting aside regular times when business talk is off limits and family members engage in activities that they enjoy together, such as hiking or sailing or travel.

Lesson 9   Family Business Student

Family businesses that succeed over time as family businesses don't do so by accident. In successful, long-lasting businesses, very often you'll find that someone during its history said, "Continuing a family business is tricky, difficult stuff. People say it can't be done. Only 30 percent make it to the next generation. We can't take this for granted. If we don't study family business as a subject and try to learn as much about it as we can, we're fools." Family business skills are not something you're born with. Like parenting skills, they are acquired, and there's knowledge to be gained and experience from which to learn.

In many of the most successful family companies I know, the leaders and other family members go to great lengths to be students of family business. As I mentioned earlier, Sam Johnson of S.C. Johnson, & Son, Inc. took a sabbatical to gain insight on how to handle ownership in the next generation.

There are simpler, less dramatic ways to study family business, however. Some families join with other family firms in family business forums, often associated with universities. This allows them to participate in educational sessions where they can absorb knowledge, think, and reflect. Such forums also give them an opportunity to meet other business-owning families and learn from their experiences.

Another way to learn is to invite members of other successful business-owning families to come and speak at your family meetings. On a routine basis, some families bring outside experts to speak at family meetings and board meetings to educate family members and board members about family business. Still other families send members out in teams to visit other family businesses and to come back and share what they learned with the rest of the family. In some families, members pass around articles on family business, or one family member may give a report on a family business book at a family meeting. One family became motivated to learn when a son who was working on an MBA did an independent research project on family business and then challenged his whole family to start learning about the subject.

Taking family business seriously as a field that can be studied and learned is a perfect example of the first of The Five Insights we talked about in Chapter 2: "We respect the challenge." When you respect the challenge, you recognize that you can't succeed at something without learning about it. Families that are committed to the continuity of their businesses into future generations are among the most likely to respect the need to educate themselves about what it takes to meet their goal.

Lesson 10   Understated Wealth

This is a very simple idea: The generation that creates the initial wealth lives beneath its means. Basically, people have two choices as to how they live with their ascending wealth. They can live lavishly and ostentatiously, or they can be understated. Being understated does not mean living in poverty or rejecting the wealth. It merely means that family members don't focus on consuming their wealth as fast as they create it.

While others of your means might have a chauffeur, you might still be in a very nice BMW. It doesn't mean you are driving a used Fiat. While you don't live in the best neighborhood you can afford, you live in the second best neighborhood you can afford. You understand that you don't have to spend or to show everything you make. Savings and prudence are not just taught at home, they are practiced.

If you do not practice the concept of understated wealth, the salaries of family members in the business can begin to escalate at a very rapid rate, which may eventually compromise the business. One of the brothers buys an island home, and all of his siblings decide they want luxurious second homes as well and they want the business (indirectly) to pay for them. To keep everybody happy, money is taken out of the business for these luxuries when the business could have retained it and used it to grow and develop. Inevitably, when there are many cousins or second cousins who have grown up expecting the lifestyle of their parents, the company suffers irreversibly.

One of the reasons it's so valuable to embrace the idea of understated wealth in Stage I is that the wealth-creating generation then adopts an attitude of saving. When founders or Owner-Managers save outside of the business, their ability to let go of control at an appropriate time is much higher because they have seen to their own financial security, and their ability to minimize tax issues is strengthened.

But most important is the effect that the concept of understated wealth has on the next generation. The family that in Stage I lives a life of slightly understated wealth, I find, has children who are more interested in the business, are more interested in work, and enjoy less expensive, less consuming interests than children from families where the senior generation is ostentatious and focused on wealth. Children from families of understated wealth tend to be better owners and better workers. They don't see money or wealth as the goal, they see it as the means to broader goals and they see it as the scorecard.

Lesson 11   Wealth is Neutral

Even though they may understate their wealth, owners of long-lasting businesses don't deny their wealth or hide it. Wealthy families are subject to one of two temptations. One is to show the wealth, display it, live it to the max. Second is to regard wealth as the source of all evil – to obsessively believe that if your children understand that the family is wealthy, they'll never work a day in their lives, or they'll be targets for kidnappers, or people will marry them for their money or take advantage of them in other ways. Some families believe the way to avoid such dire consequences is to make sure nobody knows that the family has money. But when you regard wealth as a problem, you create guilt about it, as well as paranoia. When you hide wealth, you increase the possibility of reclusiveness on the part of family members and the chance of low self-esteem among members of the next generation.

Like so many things, the treatment of wealth is a matter of balance. One family said it best: "We know we're handling our wealth well when it is a neutral concept in terms of our behavior. We're not reacting against our wealth and we're not enthralled with it, either. We don't use our wealth to curry favor, and we don't fear that our wealth means that our children will never be decent human beings."

It's important that the senior generation not deny the wealth a family has. The sooner family members understand what they really have, honestly and straightforwardly, the better. The longer information is withheld, the more massive the shock. At age 35, they may discover a great contradiction in their lives. The reaction will be an enormous sense of betrayal: "All my life, I've been told we couldn't afford this, we couldn't afford that. Didn't my parents trust me with knowing that we had money?" The answer is no, they didn't. And so, by hiding its wealth, the senior generation creates distrust, diminished self-esteem, and all sorts of contamination in the next generation.

The Wealth Is Neutral lesson means that wealth is merely a result of effort and good fortune. Share the fact that the family is wealthy with your children. Don't be embarrassed by it. Your children will live in better houses than most of their friends and might have more access to more resources at a younger age. And you can say, "We're very fortunate. Yes, we can afford it. Yes, we work hard. We've accomplished a lot, and as a result, our life is enhanced and easier." Many practice and repeat the old adage, "To whom much is given, much is expected."

A TALE OF TWO FAMILIES (CONT.)

Adolph Ochs was decidedly an entrepreneur of heroic proportions, with enormous vision for *The New York Times* and a deep sense of purpose. The *Times* was simply to become the best newspaper in the country.[11]

Although Adolph never saw his daughter as leading The New York Times Company, he shared his love of newspapering with her. When she was a child, say Tifft and Jones, "Adolph delighted in squiring Iphigene around the *Times*, introducing her to his editors and reporters and gently instructing her in the business of the newspaper."[12] Adolph understood the significance of the role that she would one day play and began to involve himself in her education. "His primary contribution," write Tifft and Jones, "... was a curriculum of his own cherished values: charity, curiosity, love of family, and the importance of protecting his prized jewel, *The New York Times*."[13]

Adolph served as both family leader and business leader. He saw himself as the "paterfamilias" and believed that his own success was the entire family's as well.[14] He often hired family members just because they were family, but he did not shrink from letting them go when he had to – he fired one brother-in-law for drinking.[15]

Adolph Ochs ran The New York Times Company from 1896 until his death in 1935 at age 77. A substantial innovator, he found a niche for the paper in factual, nonsensational reporting, introduced a Sunday illustrated magazine, and sought women readers as well as businessmen. He wasn't afraid to employ the best non-family executives he could find and reward them well. In 1904, for example, he hired a managing editor, luring him in part with an option to buy *Times* stock. At the man's death in 1945, his shares were worth $500,000, a sizeable sum at the time.[16]

With Iphigene's husband, Arthur Hays Sulzberger, in charge, The New York Times Company resembled the continuation of an Owner-Managed business – except that the Ochs trust, not Arthur, was the controlling owner.[17] What Iphigene and Arthur had to face was the fact that their four children – Marian, Ruth, Judith (Judy), and their little brother, Arthur Ochs Sulzberger Sr., known as "Punch" – would, upon Iphigene's death, inherit equally the shares in the Ochs Trust and would have to meet the challenge of joint ownership. The senior Sulzbergers enlisted the help of the family lawyer, Eddie Greenbaum. Beginning when Punch was 11, Greenbaum gathered the children together for occasional seminars on what it would mean to inherit *The New York Times*. From him, they learned that they were to avoid conflict. The family's role was one of service, they were told, and they could join the company and attain the highest levels, but they would have to do so on merit. Greenbaum taught them about stocks and trusts, say Tifft and Jones, and imbued them with a sense that the newspaper was more "a public institution than a private possession."[18]

The first of the children to marry, in 1941, was Marian. The day before the wedding, the four siblings signed the first of many documents aimed at keeping the *Times* under family control. It was a buyback agreement stipulating that they would give one another the right of first refusal if, once they had come into their inheritance, they wanted to sell their common stock.[19] Marian, the oldest sibling, was no more than 22 at the time; the two youngest were still teenagers.

Like his father-in-law, Arthur continued to bring family members into the business. Among them was his new son-in-law, Orvil Dryfoos. After a long and systematic development program, Orvil was named president in 1957 and publisher four years later, when Arthur was 70.[20]

Unfortunately, the selection of successor had to be remade two years later when Orvil died of an enlarged heart. As the two remaining trustees of the Ochs Trust, it was up to Iphigene and Arthur to make the choice. Arthur saw Punch as too young and green, but Iphigene and Punch's three sisters were in agreement that Punch should have the opportunity.[21] Finally, Arthur relented and, at the age of 37, Punch became president and publisher.

When Judge Bingham purchased *The Courier-Journal* and *The Louisville Times*, young Barry was 12. He had suffered a difficult childhood. When 7 years old, he was a passenger in an automobile with his mother when the vehicle was hit by a train and she was killed.[22] He was sent away to live with his aunt in Asheville, North Carolina, leaving him feeling rejected.[23] He was not called home until four years later, after the death of his stepmother, Mary Lily.

Eager for his father's approval, Barry joined the family business in 1930, starting at WHAS, a radio station his father had launched eight years before[24] – the same year Judge Bingham had also helped initiate a printing company, Standard Gravure.[25] Soon Barry married Mary Caperton, an intellectually gifted young woman he had met while he was a student at Harvard and she was at Radcliffe.

It would be Barry who would establish the vision of creating a great, liberal, Southern newspaper.[26] With his father, Barry made two inspired hires – Mark Ethridge, an experienced publisher, as the newspapers' general manager, and Lisle Baker, a banker, as secretary. Barry now had his own trusted managers in place and the professionalization of the Binghams' company began.[27] On his father's death in 1937, Barry, at age 31, became president, publisher, and controlling owner of the Bingham enterprises.[28]

Under the leadership of Barry Bingham and Mark Ethridge, the newspapers grew in stature, and Mary played an undeniably strong role. She became a vice-president and director of the newspapers and WHAS, wrote editorials for *The Courier-Journal*, and ran its book page.[29] Her most critical contribution, however, was as Barry's confidante and counselor and, sometimes, conscience. She often prodded him to take stronger stands than he would have otherwise.[30]

They had five children: Worth, the first, born in 1932; Barry Jr.; Sallie; Jonathan, and the youngest, Eleanor, born in 1946.

The Ochs-Sulzberger family exemplified many of the Stage I lessons – Family First Environment, the Principal of Merit, Many Non-Family Executives, and Opportunities for Wealth for those executives.

Arthur and Iphigene set the stage for the sibling partnership to come by educating their children early about the responsibilities of ownership and passing along the values that they and Adolph Ochs cherished – particularly the importance of family unity and of regarding *The New York Times* as a sacred institution. Their sense of family was profound, leading to a tradition of involving family members in the company.

The Binghams never developed a tradition of widespread family participation in the business; hence, there were no cousins or uncles or in-laws to choose from when succession planning became imperative. While the Binghams understood the lesson of Many Non-Family Executives, the idea of creating wealth for those executives didn't register. When Mark Ethridge finally retired after nearly 30 years of serving the Binghams and contributing significantly to the newspapers' finest years, it was said that he received a pension and a modest bonus. His wife was furious. "After years of loyal service," say Tifft and Jones, "she had expected the Binghams to make it possible for Mark to retire a rich man. Barry Sr., however, felt that he owed Mark only comfort and security."[31]

Neither the Binghams nor the Ochs-Sulzbergers had adopted the concepts of Irrevocable Retirement or Social Entrepreneurs. In their business's first stage, the Ochs-Sulzberger family practiced a form of Voluntary Accountability by permitting, encouraging even, *Times* reporters to write about the *Times* as objectively as they would write about other subjects (a practice that would be institutionalized by Barry Bingham Jr.). But the two families' boards of directors were made up mostly of family members and key employees, offering little opportunity for objective scrutiny.

The Ochs-Sulzbergers understood the concepts of Understated Wealth and Wealth Is Neutral. Adolph Ochs never drew more than a modest salary.[32] He was in his mid-70s before he bought Hillandale, a palatial country home that became, more than anything, a gathering place for family.[33] For his descendants, the privilege of being entrusted with an institution like the *Times* would far outweigh considerations of wealth, as later chapters will show.

Wealth was neither neutral nor downplayed in the Bingham family. Appearances were matters of great importance to Judge Bingham, who had suffered the rigors of near-poverty in the South during Reconstruction. When at last he came into his inheritance from Mary Lily, he bought a twenty-room mansion overlooking the Ohio River and transformed it into an English estate, even importing a British butler. Critics sneered at his newspapers' reporters as "the British press."[34]

While future generations of Binghams were not so ostentatious, they never shook off the hold that wealth had over them. Perhaps no one in the family understood the concept of "wealth is neutral" better than Joan

Bingham, a daughter-in-law in the third generation. The widow of that generation's heir apparent, she bitterly opposed the sale of the family's media empire. Her son and daughter would be wealthy, but to her, that was not the point. Soon after her father-in-law made the decision to sell, she wrote him a letter telling him she worried about what effect the transaction would have on her children, Clara, then 22, and Rob, 19. "Having a lot of money ... does not build character," she told him. "I still don't think my children know the satisfaction that comes from hard work ... and the money doesn't help this."[35]

5 Stage II: The Sibling Partnership

From a business perspective, the major task at the Sibling Partnership stage is the revitalization of the business's strategy. The business has gone through the founding or acquisition era, it has achieved success, it has matured, and by Stage II, after 20 to 35 years under one CEO, it has probably stagnated. But there's a secure foundation and, with the right strategy, the Stage II leaders can re-energize the company.

The most critical family issue at Stage II, however, is the capacity of the siblings to work together as a team. A weak business with a strong sibling team has good promise. A strong business with a fractured sibling team, however, is a business that's going to be in trouble. There is no greater task facing siblings than to focus on the strength and quality of their partnership. Their ability to reinvigorate the company depends on their ability to work side by side effectively.

Usually, there will be very little in the siblings' background that points them in the direction of a successful working relationship. Most sibling groups find that they have to overcome their upbringing and turn away from some of their parents' most cherished entrepreneurial instincts in order to function as a team. Founders and other dominant Owner-Managers succeed often because they are hard-charging, autocratic, incredibly decisive, and even secretive. What a business needs from a Stage II Sibling Partnership, however, is almost the opposite of what it needed during the Owner-Manager's era.

It's my personal theory that the people least likely on Earth to learn the skills of working together as a team are the children of entrepreneurial parents. Even though they may grow up in the same home with the same values, the same genetics, and the same parents, siblings tend to be very different from one another. As they develop, they are constantly trying to differentiate themselves and further their own uniqueness. And yet, if they are going have a successful Sibling Partnership in a family business, they have to somehow, miraculously, mold themselves into a team.

66

What happens when Dad, an entrepreneur who has just worked a difficult 12-hour day, comes home in the evening and finds the kids squabbling at dinner? How is the conflict resolved? As suggested in the last chapter, Dad pounds on the table, demanding peace and quiet and obedience. That, obviously, does not do much for building team skills and problem-solving experience among the siblings.

Children of entrepreneurial parents tend not to grow up in homes where conflict is accepted or where it is allowed to run its course so that the brothers and sisters can develop the skills to work it out. Instead, Dad (or Mom) exerts that powerful entrepreneurial personality and says, "This is the way it's going to be. End of discussion. Why? Because I said so!"

The practical issue here is that members of a sibling partnership have to convert from a culture with one person in control to a culture of interdependence. Consider the values typical of a founder: individualism, personal control, secrecy, and privacy. Generally, in the entrepreneur's view, "The less people know, the better it is."

But look at the values that work at the sibling partnership stage. Instead of individualism, you have to believe in collectivism. Instead of exerting personal control, you need to rely on mutual dependence. Instead of secrecy and privacy, you have to be willing to openly share information – even sensitive, personal information, such as salaries, estate plans, and investments – with your brothers and sisters.

What the sibling generation must do to assure a thriving business is often in direct contradiction to the way the business was run by the dominant Owner-Manager. Count on this fact to cause some friction between the Owner-Manager and his or her successors.

At the Sibling Partnership stage, despite the differences in the siblings' personalities and abilities, it works best when things are kept as equal as possible in terms of individual standards of living and perceptions of people's importance in the business. This is a time to minimize differences, not create them. When siblings are co-owners and partners leading a business worth $20 million, it's not worth the possible resentment that occurs when one sibling earns $25,000 or $50,000 more than another, no matter what titles they hold. I would extend this philosophy to sibling-owners who do not work in the business as well. Suppose there are two brothers and a sister who each own a third of the business. The brothers each work in the business and pull down annual salaries of $300,000 apiece. The sister is suffering financially – she's divorced, she doesn't want to work outside the home because she's got four small children to look after, and her ex-husband is unreliable about providing support. She points out one day that she can't send her kids to the same-quality schools her brothers' children can go to. She'd like to live in the same neighborhood her brothers do, but she can't afford it. She is often embarrassed when she is approached by community organizations for donations. They view her as a member of a well-known business-owning family, but the truth is, she hasn't the resources to make the contributions.

If the brothers are smart, they will recognize that there is a problem here, and they will also be mindful that their sister's children will be owners of the business one day, along with their own children. One of the ways they can address the sizable difference in their sister's standard of living is through a dividend policy that will provide her with income. Another way is to buy back some of her stock. The brothers may each end up with 35 percent of the shares and she may have 30 percent, but she will have picked up $1 million or so, enabling her to live a lifestyle closer to that of her brothers.

Siblings in a partnership need to minimize distinctions and differences and to keep things as equal among themselves as they can. At the same time, in one of family business's many contradictions, they need to begin to accept and embrace the idea of differences, in preparation for the cousin stage.

Siblings have very different personal styles – learned at a young age as they seek to differentiate themselves from one another. They develop different communication styles, different decision-making styles, and different information-processing styles. These disparities lead to inevitable conflict, as well as to different insights and complementary ways of thinking. Understanding, respecting, and managing these differences is key to a sibling partnership and requires the development of high-level communication skills.

Sibling rivalries and conflict typically break into the open shortly after the death of "Mom" – that is, the individual who serves as the family leader and holds the family together emotionally. (See Lesson 26, Successor to "Mom.") That person's moral leadership has often bridged the sibling differences and contained or suppressed the sibling conflicts. The siblings have to master the skills to cope with their differences before the death of "Mom" occurs, and it's important for "Mom" to nurture their ability to do so independently rather than to embrace their dependence on her for harmony. Once "Mom" is gone, succession of the family leadership/ emotional leadership has to take place within the sibling group as soon as possible.

Here are the lessons that need to be put in practice for Stage II, the Sibling Partnership.

LESSONS LEARNED

Essential from a Business Perspective

Lesson 12   Graceful Pruning

Business-owning families mistakenly often try to protect the business by making it exceedingly difficult and painful for family members to sell their shares. Shares are assigned a very low valuation and payments may be made only over a very long period of time, so as to make selling unattractive. Or, if family members do sell, they're made to feel like they're no longer part of the family – no more invitations to holiday gatherings, for example, or constant reminders about how Grandpa would turn over in his grave if he knew. These families reason that discouraging redemptions is better for the business because it doesn't have to come up with the money to buy out the shares, so the money is available for company growth. I find, ironically, that the more freedom of exit is available, the less family members will fight for it or even exercise it.

Far-sighted families, however, take a paradoxically different approach. They make it easy for the Stage II siblings to sell their shares in the business. They believe doing so makes sense for many reasons. In the first place, they know that in the long run, having fewer owners is easier to manage than having many owners. They also recognize that at some point, some family members are going to want to sell their shares. But if the family makes it difficult for them to sell, the business will end up with the very thing it doesn't want: some very disgruntled owners. When owners become unhappy, they start to develop hatred toward family members who kept them from selling, and the possibility of litigation increases, as well as unpleasant publicity about such litigation.

Wise families also realize that if a family member is likely to want out, it's less costly to buy him out today than later when the value of the shares has increased.

These smart families engage in what I call "graceful pruning" or "facilitated pruning." They not only make it easy for family members to sell their ownership position but they are also gracious about it. They make sure that family members understand they have the privilege of selling and won't ostracized from the family for doing so. Nor are they made to feel guilty about selling. As a practical matter, these families recognize that the sellers will be less aggressive in their negotiations when they are treated fairly and pleasantly.

Sometimes, there are siblings who you know will not be good team members or contented owners over the long term. In such cases, smart families facilitate their departure from ownership by creating the opportunity for them to very easily and comfortably sell their shares. Before they even express a desire to get out, you might say to them, "You know, a family business isn't for everybody, and that's okay. If you ever want to get out, we have these mechanisms in place to make that possible. We just want you to know they're there. And if anybody takes advantage of them, that's okay, because it has nothing to do with your membership in the family." No stigma is attached to getting out.

Perceptive families don't price the stock so cheaply that an unhappy owner can't afford to sell. Instead, a family may pay 10 percent or 20 percent more than the stock is worth to make it attractive for an individual to leave, confident that the company will grow even more in the next couple of years – especially without the distraction of unhappy owners.

It's important to understand that some family members who say they want to be owners really aren't happy as owners. They may want to be owners because it's the only way they can feel like members of the family or the only way their parents will really accept them. Or they know that if they sold, they'd get such a low price for their stock that they'd look foolish to their spouses, their families, and themselves. In such cases, the price of not being an owner is just too high.

Every family business needs a good exit clause in both its buy–sell agreement and its valuation and liquidity policy. More important, it needs a good attitude about exits – one that is generous and nonjudgmental and that proactively creates opportunities for people to exit whenever there are early signs that that's what they want to do. At the sibling stage, Graceful Pruning is a somewhat informal process. In Stage III, it becomes formalized, as you will see in Lesson 32, "Fair, Facilitated Redemption Freedom."

The ultimate goal is to concentrate ownership in the hands of people who can move the company forward because they share common interests, common goals, and common values.

Lesson 13   Leverage Strengths of Being Private

Privately held family businesses have distinct competitive disadvantages – inability to raise as much funding as public firms because of lack of access to capital markets, for example, or difficulty in attracting the best executives because they can't offer the same kind of stock option plan as their public counterparts. Even a family-controlled publicly held company will face some of the same competitive disadvantages. The family won't want to gain access to too much capital, for example, because it won't want to dilute its ownership-control position too much.

However, really successful, long-lasting family businesses are very wise about using their unique advantages as private family businesses. One of these is a long-term orientation. Family businesses don't have to gear their management practices to meet the quarterly expectations of shareholders or stock analysts. They can make decisions today that might not pay off for many years.

Family businesses are also able to make decisions and commitments more quickly, enabling them to take advantage of opportunities more bureaucratic companies might miss out on. Instead of wading through the layers of decision making typical of public companies, the family business CEO who enjoys the trust and support of her brothers and sisters can act on the spot to take advantage of a good opportunity.

Comfort with the risks of the business is another unique competency of a family firm. To owners who are involved in the business everyday and who may have even grown up with it, the risks don't seem so great. They know the business well and have developed an intuitive feel for the risks involved and know how to control them.

Still another unique strength of family businesses is trust. Family business owners seek to create trust within their organizations and in their business dealings outside the company. They build businesses that depend on trust.

As the controlling owners of a holding company whose success depends on partnerships with other companies as well as on public investment, members of the Ayala family, in the Philippines, know the value of the stability, trustworthiness, and long-range orientation that being private can provide. The Ayala Corporation, which was founded as a distillery in 1834, now maintains interests in banking, light rail, telecommunication, and other endeavors. According to Jaime Augusto Zobel de Ayala II, the seventh generation president and CEO, the parent company strives to provide the long-term vision and support that will see a partner through uncertain times, while the institutional investors push for financial returns. The two perspectives, he suggests, create a tension that enhances the odds of success.[1]

The family has an unwritten rule, for example, that family shareholders don't invest in companies competitive to Ayala. "It ensures that if a partner invests with us, it will not be competing with another entity in which a family member has an interest," says Zobel.[2]

By keeping a very low profile, a Paris-based family firm, Sonepar, has quietly acquired electrical supply companies around the globe. Today, with annual revenues exceeding €6.6 billion, operations in 29 countries and more than 19,000 employees, Sonepar is an international leader in the distribution of electrical equipment.[3] If the Sonepar name is not familiar, it's because the Coisne and Lambert families, which own it, follow a strategy of retaining the names of the acquired companies and continuing management by local people who understand the local customs. In discussing the relationship between the family holding company and its acquisitions, one of the local managers, Emmanuel Gravier, of Franco-Belge, in Malakoff, France, said Sonepar gives a great deal of freedom to its branches. "The family character of the corporation makes for a close and trusting relationship – trust that is seen by all as indispensable."[4]

In many cases, being a family-held company was a plus in Sonepar's ability to acquire other firms, because they, too, were privately held. When Sonepar sought to purchase Franco-Belge in the late 1960s, it was tough going because the owner was wary of his company being acquired and then stripped. Henri Coisne, now honorary chairman of Sonepar, recalled that Franco-Belge had been the man's "life-work, and he wouldn't have wanted to sell it to just anyone. ... We had to prove and prove again that we were worthy of his heritage and simply wished to work it, develop it and insure that it lasted over time."[5] Sonepar, founded as a textile operation in 1867, is now run by a daughter, Marie-Christine Coisne, who succeeded her father as chairman and CEO.

Lesson 14   Invest in Social Capital

What this means is investing in and creating good will in your community, however you want to define it. It can be local, regional, or even national, depending on the size and scope of the business and where it is located.

Sometimes businesses prefer to be discreet about their contributions to the community, and that's perfectly all right. However, I have found long-lasting businesses to be open in terms of providing social benefit to their communities.

This can take many forms. In some countries, family businesses create strong relationships with the community by providing schools and hospitals. One business secured its position in a small, politically volatile country by investing in and treating the company's thousands of employees extremely well and earning their support.

When family businesses invest in the social welfare of the communities around them, they receive many benefits in return. One is that they build good will that helps protect and sustain them through external changes, such as a shift in government. Because they're being good citizens, such businesses' interests are considered when government policy decisions are made – even a decision as simple as rezoning a parcel of land. They develop a positive reputation that comes back to them in terms of being able to attract employees and customers. And, finally, the business owners feel better about their ownership and proud of their company because it is making a visible, positive difference.

At Y.B.A. Kanoo in Bahrain, writes Khalid Kanoo, "Involvement in the community has always been part of our corporate 'credo' ... We believe that we should give to the community in recognition of what we have gained from it."[6] Over the years, the Kanoo family has funded youth clubs, community halls, and the building and refurbishing of 13 mosques. In the 1950s, it provided funds for the region's first nursing school, named – like the company itself – after Yusuf bin Ahmed Kanoo, the second-generation leader whose instinctual understanding of international trade is credited with the early modernization of the Kanoo family business.[7]

Freudenberg Group, a diversified family company headquartered in Weinheim, Germany, launched a unique program for young people to mark its 150th anniversary in 1999. It is called TANNER, which stands for "Travel And Navigate New Exciting Roads." The initiative not only honors the company's beginnings as a tannery, but also recognizes what the company is today: an international organization. Owned by 284 family shareholders, Freudenberg – now engaged in such businesses as seals and vibration control technology, nonwovens, and household products – employs 28,000 people in 43 countries.[8]

TANNER offers employees' children and grandchildren the chance to spend two to four weeks with the family of another employee in one of the other countries where Freudenberg is located. One of the aims of this horizon – expanding program is to prepare young people for international business life, but it also introduces them to the values of the company at which their parents and grandparents work. In addition, it reflects the business' reality. "On a daily basis," says a company statement, "Freudenberg's employees experience the importance of taking an open-minded approach to different cultures, and of showing respect and tolerance in working with other people from all over the world."[9] The TANNER program is now fully entrenched as part of Freudenberg's tradition of social responsibility, which, over the last century or so, has included the construction of a kindergarten, the donation of municipal public baths, funds for building an indoor public swimming pool, and more.[10]

To fully benefit from their social initiatives, family businesses will find that retaining public relations counsel can be very helpful. Often because successful business families take to understatement with great enthusiasm, they neglect to promote the public good that they do. The distinction is for the family to be understated as a family, but to promote the company's interests as a company fully. The business needs support and deserves it.

Lesson 15   Business Bias

Remember Lesson 8, which argued that operating the business on a Principle of Merit was good not only for the business but also for the family? This lesson operates in somewhat the same way.

I have an assessment survey that identifies a family business as a "family-first business" or a "business-first business," defining family-first businesses as those that put the family ahead of the business and business-first businesses as those that put the business ahead of the family.

The most successful family firms I've observed don't think in those terms. Instead, they synthesize the concepts of family and business and proceed on the notion that what is good for the business also serves the best interest of the family. Making decisions that are favorable to the business's vitality, strength, and longevity are not seen as being disadvantageous to the family but as important to the vitality, strength, and longevity of the family as well.

This "business bias" comes into play where decisions intersect the interests of the family and the interests of the business – such as employment policies, compensation policies, valuation, and liquidity policies, who can serve on the board, and the structure of ownership. What I have seen is that really good family businesses deliberately build a business bias into the decision-making and conflict-resolution processes. For example, let's assume there are four family members who are equal owners. However, they have a dispute and cannot come to agreement on an issue of considerable importance. They are caught in a tie over a matter that affects both family and business. Should they come down on the side of the family or the business? Faced with such a deadlock, our long-lasting family businesses would turn to a non-family CEO or to the non-family directors on the board to break the tie. In so doing, they would purposely be putting the decision into the hands of people who have an orientation toward the best interests and welfare of the business. Ultimately, business-biased decisions have a boomerang effect, coming back to serve the long-term interests of the family.

Ahmed Ali Kanoo was both the fourth-generation Y.B.A. Kanoo Group chairman and the family leader from 1952 until his death in 1997. A highly revered elder, he shaped and articulated a credo that guided the family.

While we can see the business bias in it, we can also see that it operates a
like a family code and ultimately aims to benefit the family. As his nephew
Khalid Kanoo recounted when Ahmed Kanoo was still living: "Selfishness
is something which he does not care to see. His goal is to ensure that all
family members work together for the benefit of the family company and
not themselves."[11] The family's goal is defined as "that of running a successful business."[12] Another proviso is that "the continued success of the
family company must not be jeopardised by personal ambition. If there is a
conflict of interests, then the company must come first."[13]

Codorníu, in Spain, uses a variety of checks and balances to assure the
business interests come first so that family interests are served. The family
council elects a chairman for a five-year term – someone who knows both
the family and the business well. Once the period is up, the individual may
seek to be reappointed. However, the council may choose someone else if
the members believe it would be better for the company.[14] When a family
executive does not live up to expectations, a change is made and it is
explained to the individual or the relatives that the interests of the company
must come first – in the form of a good profit – so that the entire family
benefits.[15]

Fundamental to making the "business-first" bias work is that it has been
well explained to the family, down through the decades or the generations,
that professionalism in business is a positive value for the family, one that,
in the long run, serves the family's interests best. The idea should be inculcated that the family is served best because a culture of merit, respect for
the business, objectivity, and concern for the interests of others dependent
on the business build the character of family members.

Lesson 16   Selective Family Employment

Let's start with a family business whose second-generation leader did not
learn the lesson of Selective Family Employment: Steinberg, Inc., of
Montreal. The company was founded as a tiny food store in 1917 by Ida
Roth Steinberg, a Hungarian immigrant. Her son Sam and his four brothers
transformed their mother's business into an empire that included supermar-
kets, real estate, retailing, restaurants, and sugar refining. The company was
sold 72 years after its founding for $1.3 billion, following years of bitter
family infighting.

Among the several reasons for the failure of the business to continue in
family hands was that Sam Steinberg, the dominating leader in Stage II,
hired and promoted family members at the expense of talented non-family

executives. When he finally designated his son-in-law, Mel Dobrin, as successor by naming him president, it appeared that Sam did so because he knew he could control Mel from his own role as chairman and chief executive.[16] He admitted that his son-in-law was not the most qualified person. "It may be in the best interests of this corporation to have a professional manager. But I've had so much fun building and running this business that I wouldn't deprive my family of running it."[17] As a result of the promotion, talented non-family executives with presidential aspirations began to seek opportunity elsewhere because they were sure they weren't going to find it at Steinberg, Inc.[18]

Ironically, Sam's children weren't encouraged to go into the business, even though they stood to inherit his holdings. They were girls and, in keeping with his time, Sam couldn't imagine a daughter in the business – even though his own mother had founded it. He never even encouraged his daughters to get a higher education, although the eldest, Mitzi, by this time a mother of three, persevered and got a law degree. Once she did, Sam invited her into the business. Mitzi, who was the wife of the company president, Mel Dobrin, was 42 when she joined the business in 1973. She started as a sales clerk in a money-losing department store division, but all too quickly, Sam made her general manager of the division, a responsibility for which she had no experience.[19] Things did not go well in her division or in the larger company. Steinberg, Inc. found itself struggling to keep up with new competition and changes in the industry. After Sam died in 1978, Mel was named chairman and CEO, and Mitzi, though she did not have the title of president, acted as though she did, undercutting many executives. Eventually a non-family president turned the company around after years of decline. When he threatened to leave if she didn't, Mitzi finally resigned in 1985.[20]

When the most successful family businesses develop their employment policies, they aim for a workable balance. On the one hand, they know that it's better to have a higher standard of entry into the business for family members than a lower one, for a variety of reasons – to encourage only the most competent family members to join the business, for example, and to assure that there is room for upward career paths for able, non-family employees.

At the same time, successful family firms know they don't want to be so selective that they discourage any and all family members from joining the company and aspiring to management. If there are no family members in management, after all, the business will likely cease being a family business.

On the whole, however, with each new generation successful families lean in the direction of being a little more selective when it comes to hiring family members. They may require somewhat more outside work experience than they would require of non-family employees, or a little more education. To regulate the number of family members in the business, especially if it's a growing family, they may institute rules, such as "no in-laws in the business," or they may permit only one person per couple to work in the company (and sometimes it's the in-law, not the blood relative, who gets the privilege). They may also adopt policies to discourage family members from coming and going or from having part-time jobs.

Long-lasting companies develop their employment policies thoughtfully and carefully, and with much discussion. They understand that setting the qualifications for entry a little higher for family members helps assure the business's strength and survival for the long term.

They also know that it's important to communicate to the family that one of the reasons the standards for employment are high is that the world expects more of a family member who works for a family business. That may be unfair in some ways. Nevertheless, exemplary business families say, "Because we have the privilege of owning a business, we have the burden of having to deal with the public's expectations and the employees' expectations of family members. That's one of the reasons we like to set the bar fairly high for entry into the business. We don't want to put family members into a position where they will be harmed by not being able to live up to public expectations."

Because the Ayala Corporation, in the Philippines, is partly publicly owned, only three members of the family are involved in managing it. As Jaime Zobel, the CEO and family member, explains, "We are always tightening the rules for a family member's right to be involved. What are the professional skills needed? Does the family member have a proven track record?" The CEOs of Ayala's subsidiaries and affiliates are non-family executives chosen for their ability and rewarded and promoted based on performance. To do otherwise, Zobel observes, would make it impossible to attract top talent and would "limit the growth potential of the business."[21]

Essential from a Family Perspective

Lesson 17   Open Disclosure / Transparency

The secrecy with which an Owner-Manager runs a business in its first stage of existence becomes counterproductive and dangerous in a second-stage business owned and operated by brothers and sisters. Often, an entrepreneurial parent is a very private person, one who regards an estate plan as his or her own business and who doesn't divulge company earnings or reveal employee compensation. Founders can be very protective of information they view as private.

Such secrecy, however, is harmful to a second-stage sibling partnership. It can foster mistrust among the partners and their spouses and can sow the seeds for enmity between different branches of the family that can last into the third generation and beyond. To build trust instead of mistrust, members of long-lasting family businesses practice the sensitive, difficult art of full and open disclosure with one another. Even though it goes against their wish for privacy, wise founders recognize and appreciate the need for openness in their children's generation and begin to foster it before the children take over.

Owners of the most successful family businesses demonstrate open disclosure in three major areas:

1. *Compensation, Perks, and Benefits.* In the ideal situation, when a founder is still running the company, he or she will be open with all the children about what each is earning. More typically, founders do not want to share this information for fear that when there are compensation differences, the children will have hard feelings. "Why is she getting more than me? Don't you love me?" Or, "You're paying him THAT much? I should be getting twice as much as he is for all the work I do!"

When parents shield their offspring from such knowledge, however, they set a precedent of secrecy and disinformation. It's beneficial when siblings, encouraged by their founder-parents, begin to create trust with one another by being open, sharing, vulnerable, honest, and forthright at a very early age. But this behavior is absolutely essential in the Sibling Partnership itself. When, for example, three brothers are running a family business together, they and their spouses need to know what salary each is making – whether they are all paid equally or, for whatever reason they have determined, they receive compensation that differs. When everyone has the information, no one is guessing at it or making more of an issue of it. In any case, when siblings control and run a company, they see the financial statements, and knowing what each other makes in salary won't be traumatic. The same openness should apply to perks and benefits. A parent who is CEO, for example, will not offer a special perk to a son or daughter – a trip to Hawaii or support for a new home – in secret. By being open about such things, the parent sets the stage for the successor CEO to be similarly open in dealings with his or her sibling partners.

2. *Outside Investment Opportunities.* Siblings who are partners in successful family businesses find it essential to share information with one another about investment opportunities they come across and about their

own personal investments. Making the group aware of promising investments offers evidence of commitment to the group as a whole, while open discussion of personal investments or a desire to make an investment keeps everyone in the know in the event an investment affects – or can have an effect on – the business.

Consider this example: Joel H., as the CEO of XYZ Company, has been invited to sit on the board of the local bank. At a luncheon after one of the board meetings, one of the other directors takes him aside and says, "Joel, here's a great opportunity. Some people I know are going to build a hotel by the river. Why don't you get in on it early with us? We can do very well."

In one scenario, Joel can put up some of his own money privately, but if he gets rich off the deal, his brothers and sisters will have some questions for him. When he tells them he invested in the new hotel, they may ask, "Why weren't you spending all your time running our company?" When he says he was a passive investor, they may say, in disbelief, "You were so passive that you didn't go to any meetings or read any reports or make any phone calls on company time?" When Joel insists he really was passive, they'll ask, "How did you find out about the hotel going up?" And when Joel admits he came by the information at the bank board meeting, his siblings will kindly remind him that the only reason he's on the bank board is that he's CEO of the family business. "You're supposed to represent all of us," they'll say. "You mean you heard about this terrific opportunity and you didn't tell the rest of us about it?"

In a second scenario, one that Joel would have been wiser to follow, he responds differently when he's approached to invest in the new hotel. He says, "Thanks a lot for inviting me. Do you mind if I share the opportunity with my brothers and sisters? We'll go in together – to whatever extent each wants to." When he's assured that it's all right to ask his siblings, he goes back to them, tells them about the opportunity, and says, "I want to put as much money as I can into this thing, but I want each of you to have an equal opportunity to participate with me if you wish." The others can choose to join in or not, but the point is, they have the chance. In this case, the opportunity that one sibling found for an investment is shared, as it should be, with all the other siblings, openly and equally.

Suppose all Joel's brothers and sisters declined the opportunity, saying they felt it was too risky. Joel could then say, "I would still like to invest. Do you mind if I do?" They might say, "We don't mind. Please go ahead." On the other hand, they might raise some legitimate concerns. Managing the investment may take a lot of time and distract Joel from running the family business. If the person overseeing the hotel project messes things up, the siblings may point out, then Joel – because he has so much money invested – may be tempted to step in and try to save the project in order to save his investment. Through such discussion, the sibling-partners may persuade Joel that he could be putting himself in a position where there's a conflict of interest between his personal investment and the family's collective welfare.

Siblings also need to be open about more ordinary investments. When they are, it eliminates the guessing and wondering that occur when some-one hits it big. It avoids the situation where a sibling or a spouse wonders how Fiona can afford that extraordinary new house or Jude can suddenly manage to take his whole family to Tahiti on vacation.

Another reason to share such information is that investments, if they go sour, impact the way the partners participate in the business. If instead of backing a winner one brother finds himself in a financial crunch, his sib-lings will know that dividends are going to be more important to him for a while and they can plan accordingly.

3. *Personal Estate Plans.* It's important for each of the brothers and sis-ters to know what the others' personal estate plans are. If one sibling is passing her stock on to her children very aggressively, there may be no taxes to pay when she dies. If another is not, there may be a huge tax bill due at death. One sibling may be giving stock only to his male children, while another is giving stock to both males and females – a situation that may explode in the third generation when the young women in one branch of the family discover they have been deprived of ownership.

When estate plans are not shared, the sibling partners and other family members will be uncertain about the long-term viability of the company because of death taxes. In addition, the siblings run a greater risk that they are creating distinctions among the cousins that may someday erupt.

Ideally, the siblings will not only share information about estate plans with one another but will be in concurrence on a philosophy about estate planning. For example, all agree to give stock to both males and females, to give voting and nonvoting stock equally to all children (instead of giving all voting stock to one child), to fund death taxes outside of the stock, and so on. If siblings cannot agree on a philosophy of estate planning or can agree on only a few different principles (And that's all right!), it becomes all the more important that they share estate planning information with one another.

As an example, Herbert Fisk Johnson Sr., the second-generation leader of S.C. Johnson & Son, had two children, Herbert Jr. (known as HF) and Henrietta. Herbert Sr., died unexpectedly at age 60 but left no will. It took 10 years for ownership matters to be sorted out. In the end, HF received two-thirds of the business shares and management control, while Henrietta was awarded one-third of the shares.[22]

Fortunately, Henrietta and HF and their families were close. At HF's urging, with the help of skillful advisers, the two families worked together to each set up three similar trusts – one to distribute dividends, one that held voting power for the business, and a third that held a large percentage of each family's shares. The plans also accounted for continuity of the business, with HF in his will naming his son Sam as successor to company leadership. By doing this kind of joint planning, Henrietta and HF not only assured a smooth transition of the family business to the next generation but also spared their children the 10 years of anguish they went through in settling their father's estate.[23]

Open disclosure goes beyond just the siblings who are working in the business. There should be complete sharing of information with sibling owners who do not work in the business – through shareholders meetings or family meetings. They should be informed on such matters as compensation, profits, and the like. Some sibling groups find it helpful to engage in open disclosure with spouses as well.

Successful family businesses also often come down on the side of open disclosure to non-family executives. While a case can be made for privacy and discretion in some situations, in general, the more information you can share with more people, the better. It works something like the Principle of Merit in that the more information it discloses, the more the family is holding itself accountable. Disclosure also has other benefits – it helps dispel the perception that the family is getting rich off the business. And when family owners share information with key non-family executives, they set a precedent for those executives to share information with their direct reports, which enhances the ability of the direct reports to contribute to the business.

Lesson 18   Aggressive Gifting

As soon as possible, as much as possible, give away the stock you own in the family business to future generations. Begin gifting shares as much as you can and as soon as you can to infants, to trusts for future-born children, and so on. The more aggressive you are in your gifting, the less your death taxes will be. At some point, all family businesses in countries where there are significant death taxes face a serious death-tax crisis. The best and cheapest way to avoid the tax for the longest period of time is to give away as much ownership as possible as early as you can to future generations. The less you hold in your own name and the least amount of time you hold it, the less the tax will be.

In the United States, where individuals can annually give away $11,000 each to as many people as they wish without paying gift taxes, couples often think it's aggressive gifting to jointly give $22,000 a year to each of their children. But more aggressive gifting would be to give $22,000 a year to each of your children *and* $22,000 a year to each of your grandchildren, and perhaps to nephews and nieces.

In addition to making use of annual tax-free gifts, business owners in the United States should also consider moving up their use of the estate tax exclusion usually taken at death – $1 million as of this writing but due to increase to $3.5 million in 2009. The sooner you use your exemption, the better, because it means less appreciates in your name.

Once they have used up their exemption and have given $22,000 in shares to as many family members as they wish, many, many successful business-owning couples in the United States find it to be a very smart idea to give even more shares and pay the gift tax because, the way they are calculated, gift taxes are much cheaper than death taxes. And, again, they know that shares that appreciate in their name mean much higher taxes later. A business owner, for example, may gift ownership of a business worth $10 million now to his children and pay perhaps $5 million in gift taxes – half of what is passed on. If he dies possessing a business worth $10 million and $5 million in cash, then the death tax is about $7.5 million – half of all that is in the estate. But much worse, if he holds on to the business and it increases in value to $50 million by the time he dies 20 years later, the tax will be around $25 million.

Obviously, aggressive gifting requires some complicated calculations and the help of a good tax advisor. It also assumes that the business owners have taken care to build some wealth outside of their business so that their needs for personal financial security are met.

Often, in my experience, the business can endure poor estate planning by the controlling owner. The business is usually smaller and it has a conservative balance sheet to finance debt for taxes, and the single owner has lived a relatively modest lifestyle.

In the succeeding generation, however, the multiple sibling owners need to focus on aggressive estate planning immediately. The growth in the business's value and the growing appetite for liquidity within the family and the disparate possible attitudes on estate planning among the siblings make surviving that generation without aggressive gifting most unlikely.

Ideally, the aggressive gifting starts in the founding generation to begin conserving capital and to set the philosophic precedent. Like all the lessons in this book, the sooner it's started, the better. But it's essential that the sibling generation embrace this concept.

Lesson 19   Next Generation Early Education

Many of the young people who are interested in and enthusiastic about going into the family business are those who have had exposure to the business from a very early age. During Stage I, children almost can't escape exposure to the business. That's all they ever hear about from their parents, and, more likely than not, they are expected to join it when they are old enough.

By Stage II and Stage III, however, parents have to make a conscious effort to create opportunities for educating young children about the business. They may also have to temper their fear that exposing the kids to the business is tantamount to putting pressure on them to choose it as a career. If the previous generation pushed them into joining the business, they don't want to brainwash their own kids into making the same choice, and they bend over backward to avoid doing so. They may even shelter the children from having any interaction with the business.

Several other factors come into play by the second and third stages: The business is successful. The family is wealthy, and the third-generation youngsters are growing up in an atmosphere of affluence – attending soccer camps, taking music lessons, and the like. By this time, some members of the family don't even live in the community where the business is located. It's very possible at this stage that many family members get virtually no exposure to the business as they grow up because they don't work in it or they live in another town.

However, even though the children may never work in the business, it is possible they will become owners. And you want them to be proud and interested owners who understand and value their heritage. In order to make that happen, you need to instill in them an appreciation for the business. You can do this by giving them a taste of the business – from an early age – in thoughtful, positive, and enjoyable ways. You can begin when they are age 8 or 9, or even younger, and continue with age-appropriate activities as the children grow older.

In one of my favorite examples, a newspaper-owning family arranged a tour of the business for a dozen children from the youngest generation. All were under the age of 12 and they came from all branches of the family. In the press room, one child, whose name was drawn out of a hat, got to push the button that started the printing press. And what should come out but a special four-page private edition of the newspaper, complete with pictures of the children and a story about their visit to the plant!

In another excellent example, a retail family took the youngsters on a train ride to attend a new store opening. The children were treated to a before-opening tour, saw a videotape of townspeople proclaiming the importance of the new store to the community, and participated in the ribbon-cutting ceremony.

When the kids are old enough, perhaps 14 to 16, employees from the business can be invited to family meetings to make presentations to them about the business. Again, these need to be cleverly handled. If you're a food company, you can have product tastings for the kids. If you're a manufacturing company, you can put your products on a table side by side with competitors' products and have the young people compare and evaluate them.

As they grow older, your children can do paid work in the company. Often, you'll find that the most committed adults in a family business like to tell stories of the grunt work they did as teenagers – cleaning up the yard or helping unload the delivery truck.

Successful business families also find it useful to begin educating their sons and daughters in family process at a relatively young age, even as young as 12 to 14. This means educating them in skills that are important to the family – such as managing inherited wealth and interpersonal skills like listening and communicating. There are also games that parents can play with children to spark their interest in entrepreneurship and even accounting. Loyola University Chicago's Family Business Center regularly invites in a speaker who teaches children as young as six about business and in no time has them giving little talks about their families' companies and products.

Educating children about their family's business is not the same as pressuring them to join it. Positive exposure encourages their pride in a company they may have ownership in someday, whether or not they work in it. By exposing your children to the business and not sheltering them from it, you give them the real freedom to choose their future by making sure they have enough information about the company on which to make an informed decision whether to embrace it or pursue a different goal. Paradoxically, the earlier the exposure coupled with no pressure to join, the more likely they will join someday.

Lesson 20   Family Code

If the business-owning family has not developed a family code in Stage I, it's essential to do so in Stage II. Typically in Stage II, family members for the first time have to grapple with the issue of how they are going to work together without leaning on parental authority to guide their behavior.

A family code, or code of conduct, is basically an agreement that states how family members will treat one another and how they will conduct themselves with the world outside the family. It is often simple in the beginning, but as the family gets older and larger, it takes on many dimensions.

A family may start with a meeting code, with such rules as: "We start on time and we end on time." "We respect each other." "We will be prepared."

The meeting rules might then be expanded into a code of interpersonal behavior, with such provisions as: "I won't interrupt." "If the situation gets too intense, I have a right to call a time-out."

As families develop their family codes, they address such questions as: How will we work together? How do we handle communications? What should our decision-making process be? How do we handle disagreements? How should we handle public relations and exposure to the public? Should we handle our philanthropy anonymously or be open about it? Some family codes include provisions calling for the sharing of estate plans with siblings and children.

One value of a family code is that it helps increase the family's attention to and appreciation of individuality. In doing so, it helps the family express respect for the individual and protect one another's dignity and rights.

A family code also helps assure that behavior is something that is mutually agreed upon rather than imposed by more powerful people or senior people. It empowers the family to take responsibility for itself.

Family codes make families far more conscious of the importance of effective communication. And finally, they provide a safety valve for the family and for family members. The safety issue is a crucial one because family meetings and family interactions are often very emotional, very challenging, very trying, and very fatiguing. A code provides guidelines for more constructive and productive interactions and is empowering in the sense that it suggests that family members are agreeing on the principles together.

The members of one large third-generation Asian family business worked very hard to develop family harmony and strength. They met three times a year for two or three days at a time – twice, to concentrate on business matters and to discuss family issues as needed, and once, to focus exclusively on the health and future needs of the family.

The central core of their philosophy, their mutual understanding, and their family strength, they believe, is their family code. They call it the "6C's." While it's verbal and not written, it is reinforced at each family meeting. My interpretation of it is in the following Table 5.1.

Other family codes are shorter and simpler. They may pledge that family members will respect one another, do what they say they will do, be ethical, be transparent, contribute to society, and so on. The key is that family members work on the statement together and come to consensus on what it says.

Table 5.1　　*The 6C's: a family code*

1. *Cash*: Liquidity is essential for business growth and unexpected family needs. We believe all [parties] profit under the profit motive. While we list "cash" first not to underestimate its importance, it is really the result of the other C's ...
2. *Communication*: Good communications are essential. We promise each and every family member an equal voice, irrespective of age. We don't need to vote. Those who are quiet are encouraged, even asked to comment. We've found those who remain quiet in a meeting are often in disagreement and will talk, away from the meeting, of their displeasure. We emphasize the important of *never closing channels*, so therefore ...
3. *Criticism*: Criticism must be constructive and intended to help the other person. We never want to "attack the person," only to discuss the concept. We find it better for uncles or elders to offer such criticism. But to be willing to accept criticism requires ...
4. *Commitment*: We are committed to the family philosophy. Commitment requires that each family member have a comfortable living. We are committed to affording and encouraging the best education the person's talents permit. We are committed to caring for one who has needs. We have a special family fund for that purpose. That's one of the purposes of "cash." So we feel deeply about ...
5. *Compassion*: We seek to be compassionate to family members and to those who work for us. We respect older family members. We give them love, time, and recognition. Sharing recognition is important because it means giving ...
6. *Credit*: We want to be humble and share. We never let anyone, however brilliant, take all the credit. We also find ways in which the family – past and present – contributed to the success of any one individual. And when one feels he's achieved a great success, he's eager to share it with others.

Lesson 21　　Communication Skills

The most successful business families I know invest a great amount of time and effort into learning communication skills, and they find it very, very powerful to learn these skills together.

The No.1 topic of families that have family meetings with an educational focus is the subject of listening skills. Effective listening is an especially critical communication skill for a family because it builds trust and creates mutual support. When you are a good listener, that lets other people feel important and helps draw out the benefits of diversity in the family. Families who learn listening skills quickly discover that the greatest obstacles to effective listening are the assumptions we have at the beginning of a conversation or an interaction. And every communication between and among family members is loaded with assumptions: "I know who you are. I know all your body language. I know how you think. I know where you're heading." As family members, we tend to quickly react based on our assumptions before we hear the content of the other person's message. But as we gain listening skills, we learn to consciously put our assumptions aside and pick up the subtlety and richness of the other person's differing perspective and add it to our thinking.

Some families work to nurture another dimension of communication – family members' presenting skills. When family members know how to get their points across effectively and succinctly, their good ideas are less likely to be passed over because of an unfocused presentation. Improving family member's presenting skills also helps family, board, and foundation meetings function better because people aren't rambling.

Other families focus on developing confrontational skills, so that they can handle disagreements in as constructive a way as possible. When a family learns confrontational skills, it becomes possible for family members to talk about difficult, even explosive, issues and to feel safe in doing so because they have developed a methodology that everyone follows and accepts.

Still another communications area that families give attention to is meeting management and facilitation skills. They want to know how to draw out participants, check for consensus, and recap a meeting.

Fortunately, there are many wonderful resources for learning communication skills – including professional facilitators and trainers. Many university communications departments are staffed with experts who can provide such training. A number of programs videotape participants so they can observe how they listen or see what their body language is like.

What's wonderful is when families learn communication skills as a group, rather than sending one member or another off to this course or that. When you do it together, you develop a common language, a common vulnerability, and a mutual support system.

The wisest families know that getting communications training isn't something you just do once. The family's communication skills need renewal as new family members come into the family process, such as next-generation family members becoming young adults or in-laws coming into the family. Many families, I find, return to some form of communications training about every three years for a refresher.

Lesson 22   Financial "Nest Eggs"

One of the most unusual lessons I've learned from wealthy business families is the value of making sure that family members who are playing very essential roles in the family or in the business have a sense of financial independence and security. What this entails is seeing to it that by the time they reach young middle age, they have their own substantial financial nest egg, with the understanding that they have the right to manage it themselves and are not accountable to anyone for it. They may make investments as they see fit or spend it without having to answer to anyone for their decisions.

What having a nest egg does for these family members is give them the opportunity to make free choices. It provides them dignity by making them feel that they're respected and that they have their own individuality, and it reassures them that they're not being controlled. It frees them from being dependent on the paternalism of the senior generation and the business, and it enables them to determine whether or not they're doing what they're doing because they are truly enthusiastic about it.

You may think of others but let me suggest three categories of individuals whose independent financial security strengthens the family and the business:

Spouses. Usually, but not always, this means wives. Even when a couple is doing well as a couple, the non-breadwinning spouse or the subordinate breadwinner in a marriage typically never feels that she has her own discretionary money to do with as she wishes. Even spouses of very wealthy entrepreneurs often don't have their own nest egg. Yet a nest egg for a spouse, particularly the non-working spouse of a successful,business-oriented person, is very appropriate. Providing one begins to reduce the culture of control and to enhance a culture of democracy. Nest eggs also help spouses feel better about themselves, thereby giving them added strength to accept differences and decisions that do not go their way.

The business founder can set an example by creating a nest egg for his spouse. Then he can create a nest egg for each of his children and encourage them in turn to create nest eggs for their own spouses, perhaps helping them to do so (but not providing a nest egg directly to a son – or daughter-in-law).

Next-Generation Business Leaders. Granted, you may be making millions of yen a year as the 45-year-old second-generation president of a family business, but if you don't have a nest egg on the side, you may not have the freedom to choose whether you want to be president or not. Successful families want family members working in the business – particularly those who are in very difficult, burdensome, leadership roles – to feel like they're there by choice. They should not be there to make a living. Most such leaders are wealthy on paper, but if they don't have discretionary funds, they don't have the chance to say, "I don't want to be the president anymore. I accepted this role because I felt obligated, but now I'm beginning to really realize that I don't want to be here."

I find that successor-leaders who have a nest egg, even if they're not having doubts about staying in the family business, are better leaders because they feel more secure about themselves and about their judgment.

Family Members who are Shareholders but who are Not Involved in the Business. Unless family shareholders have money of their own outside the business, they are going to feel very dependent on their parents and on the business. And whenever issues arise about dividends or shareholder liquidity, family members who are independently secure will be concerned that the dependent owner is just in it for the money or worried about himself. The dependent shareholder may start to question himself and wonder, "Am I being selfish here?" It's very hard to be committed to the long-term good of the company when dividends and liquidity are your lifeline. It's better for both the family and the business that family shareholders have independent financial security so that they can voluntarily support decisions that strengthen the business rather than act out of fear for their own well-being.

The concept of nest eggs is a controversial one, and many families have trouble with the idea. Having financial independence will mess up the work ethic, they cry. Senior-generation family members, especially founders, may be judgmental and even resentful, saying, "Nobody deserves any money unless they have earned it." And, indeed, the founders really did work very hard for every centime.

However, the rules change in Stage II and Stage III, when younger family members have to learn to accept wealth and to feel good about themselves, and have the opportunity to choose to participate in the business or not. What I have seen is that financial independence doesn't cause people to be irresponsible. It gives them the freedom to learn from their mistakes and to make decisions on their own.

One of the real issues in family businesses, especially in the early generations, is the question of individuality and independence. "Am I independent?" younger family members want to know. "Can I make my own decisions? Am I trusted and believed in as an individual?" When they have financial independence, they think more clearly and freely, they feel much more strength as an individual, and they feel empowered. In some families, that's precisely what some other people don't want. They want, instead, to use financial dependence as a control mechanism.

Successful families don't do that, however, because they recognize there are dire consequences. When parents use financial dependence to manipulate next-generation family members, for example, they create low self-esteem, anger, and repressed bitterness in those being controlled. When the parents are no longer around, things can explode. The younger people take their anger out on the business, on the successor, or on older employees or family members who may have supported their parents in their use of financial dependence as a control technique. The next-generation family members, having been deprived of the opportunity to manage their own money and learn from their mistakes in doing so, will have developed no financial capacity. Instead of being more responsible, as their parents expected, they are more irresponsible.

Where are the nest eggs to come from? They come from the business in the form of special dividends or distributions, or they come from the generosity of the senior generation. And, of course, there is a price to pay. If a nest egg comes from the business as a special distribution, that's money the business could have used to grow. If it comes from the parents, that means parents have had to gift cash instead of gifting stock and saving death taxes on the stock transition. It's tempting to argue against the nest-egg concept on the basis of taxes or business strategy. But successful families refuse to think about the issue only from a tax perspective or a business perspective. They are so committed to the extraordinary benefits of having liberated, empowered owners that they are willing to make the tough trade-offs necessary to make nest eggs possible.

While it's desirable that family members be encouraged at relatively young ages to take some responsibility for their savings, that's usually not enough to achieve the kind of financial independence required here. We're talking about a significant amount of money, and in the second and third generations, there will be family members whose compensation does not give them enough money or time to gather the nest egg on their own.

Lesson 23   Shared Investments

Sharing investment opportunities is so prevalent among strong sibling teams that it seems almost instinctive. This lesson reflects some of the points embedded in Lesson 17, "Open Disclosure" – for example, that disclosing investment opportunities to one another demonstrates commitment to the sibling group.

However, there are more reasons why successful sibling teams share investment information and often invest together. They know that the more one member of the team takes advantage of investments, however legitimate, the more it creates personal wealth for him and exacerbates the differences in standards of living among the siblings. The more the sibling generation struggles with financial differences among themselves, the more difficult it is to hold a sibling team together.

Strong sibling teams also recognize that there is a trust-building dimension to sharing investment opportunities with one another. When one sibling tells the rest of the group about an excellent investment opportunity she has come across, she displays a generosity of spirit and conveys the attitude that she is looking out for the best interests of the whole family. It's an attitude that says, "Wouldn't it be nice if we could all be better off, if we could all be more liquid and more diversified and more successful?"

Instilled in these sibling teams is a spirit of being a family in enterprise together and of eagerly and enthusiastically – for many good reasons – sharing in investment opportunities together. It doesn't mean that somebody must participate if they don't want to – some members of the group may feel that they can't afford to invest at a particular time. But I've seen some families where one sibling will invest for another with his own money, believing that in the long run, the individual who said he wouldn't participate will be happier being a partner even though in the short run, he has chosen not to. And because it's done with such a gracious spirit, the gesture is not seen as patronizing nor is it resented.

Lesson 24   Educate In-laws

A business-owning family needs the in-laws to be supportive of the family and its enterprise. One of the best ways to earn this support, successful families have found, is to thoughtfully and sensitively educate in-laws as they come into the family.

There are three areas where in-laws can use your help: (1) Understanding the family from a cultural point of view – its history and traditions and how the family thinks; (2) Learning the nature of the business, such as what makes the business tick, how to read financial statements, what a board of directors does, and how estate plans are handled; and (3) Indoctrination into the family's process. The in-law may be expected to participate in family meetings, or perhaps the family has been having communications training experiences like the ones we discussed under Lesson 21, "Communication Skills." In-laws need to be brought up to speed in the language and in the skills of the family.

More often than not, the education of in-laws is an informal but deliberate and well-planned process. Like a mentor, someone – a matriarch, a family council, a family elder or other family leader – takes the new in-law under his or her wing. Sometimes, other in-laws will take on this role because, as they can say, "We've been through it. We've been here before."

The mentor sees to it that the new in-law is taken on a tour of the business, meets the board of directors, and gets personally introduced to each of the family's advisors. A good advisor may invite the in-law to lunch just to get acquainted and to open the door for more specific discussions later. For example, encouraged by the family, a financial advisor will educate the in-law about the assets that are involved, how the family does its estate planning, how the dividends work, and agreements the family has on family compensation or family liquidity.

The family mentor will also pave the way for the in-law to attend seminars, workshops, and conferences with other family members on such topics as family business, family foundations, and family offices.

The wise family understands that new family members feel awkward and uncomfortable. They are likely to be shy and probably won't ask to meet the advisors or board members. Though they are understandably curious, they will attempt not to appear nosy. So it's up to the family to take the lead in providing in-laws with information and education. And the more they learn and the sooner they learn it, the more quickly they will become active participants in the family and supporters of its central undertaking, the business.

In any case, in-laws aren't just extra family members. Family businesses are often managed by in-laws. According to researchers Christine Blondel and Ludo Van der Heyden, the Wendel family in France has survived since 1704 as a business-owning family in part because at certain points in its history, in-laws, including women, stepped in to run its enterprises.[24] The business started with forges in Lorraine; today Wendel Investissement is an international holding company with interests in industrial abrasives, biotechnology, and information technology.[25]

Lesson 25   Legacy of Values

The idea of passing on a value system is fundamental to the most successful business-owning families. Many families with businesses believe that one of the things that make families important is that they are able to instill values in the next generation. For them, one of the reasons business ownership is worthwhile is that it provides an opportunity for passing on values. They come to recognize that the business is a concrete, tangible, real-world arena where the family's values are tested and are proven to have worth.

Nowhere is the synergy between family and business as clear as it is in the realm of values. The values come from the family and are applied to the business. They may include integrity, persistence, openness, respect for and caring about people, trust with customers and suppliers, and a belief in entrepreneurial spirit. As the values are seen to really make a difference and serve the business, enhancing its success, they bring strength back to the family because it can use the business as a mirror and as a reminder that the family's values really do have merit.

One of the things a family business needs to do, then, is to serve as an example of the family's values. It can show the family how its values work in the business and how they make a positive impact. Contrarily, the business world can demonstrate how absence of values – lack of integrity, for example – can have a deleterious effect.

Ultimately, family members become more interested and committed as owners because the business stands for something that really makes a difference to the family (and, most likely, to the community). Their desire to pass the business on to future generations is strengthened because they see the business as a transmitter or living example of values.

More than just being consistent with the family's values, the business actually contributes to the family's values in return. Successful families are not only focused on how to perpetuate their value system, but are thoughtful, pro-active, and imaginative about how values pass back and forth between the family and the business for the benefit of both. One family, for example, has a very strong belief in integrity and ethics. As a result, the business has developed a code of ethics that goes beyond the codes of ethics of most companies. It bars employees from accepting even small gifts from suppliers at Christmas or participating in supplier golf outings because it doesn't want even the slightest perception of inappropriate influence. Thus the values of integrity and ethics that originated with the family are passed on to and applied to the business. In turn, the family reinforces the values at occasional family meetings by sharing examples of how the code of ethics works or reading letters the business has received from customers and vendors praising the company for its integrity.

Before this kind of conscious interaction can take place between family and business, however, a family must be able to articulate its value system. This is not always easy because when families ask, "What are our values?" they often come up with responses that are generic and uninspiring. But the process of thinking about values and trying to draw them out can be fun, productive, and insightful. Two exercises can help. In one, family members interview people outside the family who know the family and the business. They might be non-family employees or people in the community who are asked to identify what they perceive the family's values to be. Such outsiders' views may turn up some surprises and give family members some stimulating perspectives to think about and discuss.

Table 5.2   *Family values statement*

As a family, we value excellence, love, trust, respect, and honor. We strive to:

- Act with integrity
- Promote self-esteem
- Teach "sense of family"
- Pursue the love of work
- Cherish individuality, independent thinking, and freedom of choice
- Encourage the participation and empowerment of every family member
- Commit to communication and the resolution of conflicts
- Serve as responsible "role models" of productive and creative people
- Create wealth responsibly and confront the challenges of wealth
- Acknowledge excellence as a personal expression, with freedom to learn from mistakes
- Demonstrate pro-active compassion and generosity
- Focus energy on the enhancement of our community
- Create an environment for lifelong learning

All these we will pass on and teach from generation to generation.

Another approach that can generate discussion and provide enjoyment is to invite family members to tell stories in a group setting. Going around a table or around a room, each family member relates the story that he or she finds most memorable or meaningful from personal experience or family lore, and then talks about what he or she thinks is the value or moral or message of that story.

These exercises encourage an "outward-in" way of looking at values and produce more imaginative results than an "inward-out" approach that starts with trying to name the values. Once the family has agreed upon its values, they can be committed to paper in a "Family Statement of Values" or "Family Creed," as in this example (see Table 5.2).

Lesson 26   Successor to "Mom"

"Mom," in this case, means the person who plays the role of the family leader. In the founding generation, this extremely important role usually falls to Mom – with the notable exceptions as *The New York Times* family in the United States and the Smorgon family in Australia, where the first-generation business leaders, Adolph Ochs and Norman Smorgon, held large, extended families together. In succeeding generations, as we shall see, the position has little to do with gender.

One of the things that sets long-lasting, successful family businesses apart is that they understand and acknowledge the role of family leadership and plan for its continuity. They recognize the many important functions that family leaders perform: keeping channels of communication open; nurturing people; making sure everyone in the family is treated fairly, if possible; seeing to it that traditions and ceremonies are attended to; reinforcing values; acculturating new in-laws to the family and the business; making certain that younger family members are educated about the business; providing moral cohesion, and serving as a mediator.

Too often, in the first stage, family members are not conscious of the role of family leadership or they don't think it's a critical role and they don't pay attention to it. All the while, Mom or someone else may be providing fantastic but subtle family leadership that may be virtually invisible to family members dazzled by the business leader – that powerful, dynamic, charismatic, popular, bigger-than-life personality. Family leadership is there, but is unseen or taken for granted.

However, when the family leader dies and family leadership disappears, families begin to drift apart. Often, conflict – especially sibling rivalry – erupts.

What long-lasting business families understand is that just as you have to plan for business leadership succession, you also have to plan for family leadership succession. One way to begin is to talk, as a family, about what family leaders do and why the family leadership role is critical. The family can then look at different models for continuing the role and determine which is most appropriate. In some families, the successor to family leadership is another individual. In others, it might be a council of elders, the chairman of the family council, the family council itself, or, informally, one or two family members who naturally take on the role but who need acceptance, acknowledgment, recognition, and support for what they are doing.

Successful families watch out for the development of unhealthy rivalries over who is going to be the family leader, which often occur in the second generation. Some individuals may desire the role for the wrong reasons – such as an enhanced feeling of importance. Family leadership needs to be seen not as a power position but as a serving position.

When I have asked them what makes them successful, a number of exemplary sibling teams have told me that their parents – sometimes on their deathbed – entreated the siblings to imagine themselves as the bundle of sticks in one of Aesop's fables. If you take a bunch of sticks together, you can't break them, the story goes. But if you take the sticks one at a time, they snap. One father, Abdurrahman B. Paksoy, founder in 1951 of Paksoy Tic San A.S., a food manufacturing firm in Adana, Turkey, put it in a similar fashion in a letter of advice to his seven sons: "Above all, remember: It is easy to snap one yarn, but ten together are not easy to break."[26]

Sibling partnerships succeed not only when they draw strength from their togetherness but also when they regard themselves and one another as equal as siblings and equal as co-owners. Even so, one member of the team often emerges and is acknowledged as a more natural, gifted business leader than the others. The key to success in this very common situation is that the person who emerges sees his leadership position as a servant leader rather than as a chief. The servant leader takes the attitude of "I'm here to make sure that my brothers and sisters are successful," rather than, "I'm here to tell these people what to do or expect."

Successful sibling teams make it a point to learn how to resolve conflicts. While some families avoid or minimize conflict by giving each sibling a "business within the business" to run (Janice gets this store, Alex will oversee that one, Jack gets a new venture), wise sibling teams tend not to rely on a system that produces fiefdoms. They know fiefdoms undermine the concept of "We are one family" and encourage the development of loyalty to one's own branch of the family that can be so damaging to future generations. Successful sibling teams choose to co-own rather than just co-exist.

Let me offer one more image of what it means to be a sibling team. Once, in India, in a discussion with members of a family business that was run by five siblings, all co-owners and co-CEOs, I observed that the siblings were all very different and asked how they could work together in this very successful business. "We see ourselves like the fingers on a hand," they replied. "Some of us are taller and stronger than others. Some of us are more dexterous. Some of us have more power. Some of us can't really do much without the others. Some of us are a little smaller and less able. But try doing anything without all five fingers and you quickly discover that each finger does make a contribution."

A TALE OF TWO FAMILIES (CONT.)

Intelligent, wealthy, and powerful, Arthur and Iphigene Sulzberger and Barry and Mary Bingham led demanding social lives that often meant leaving the children at home in the care of others. But the two groups of young people reacted differently to their parents' absences. The Sulzberger children banded together against a hated governess.[27] The Binghams fought among themselves for their parents' love and attention. These patterns of the Sulzberger siblings uniting and the Bingham children wrangling with one another carried over into adulthood. Let's look at the Binghams first this time.

Mary and Barry Bingham Sr. were so deeply in love all their lives that some friends thought their relationship shut out the offspring. "You know what they say," commented one family acquaintance. "The closer the parents, the more orphaned the children."[28]

Barry Sr. left Mary to do the heavy lifting of discipline, dealing with boarding school headmasters, and correcting the children's manners. "Mother has a tongue that could take your skin off," Sallie once said of the criticism she received as a child.[29]

In their attempt to win some closeness with their parents, the Bingham children divided into factions: the two oldest, Worth and Barry Jr. formed one alliance, and the two youngest, Eleanor and Jonathan, another. Sallie, the middle child, was left to fend for herself. From childhood, Sallie saw Worth as a bully and as her enemy.[30]

As the firstborn, Worth Bingham was the family business's heir apparent. Rebellious as a teenager, he barely scraped his way through Harvard.[31] But several newspaper apprenticeships and his marriage to Joan Stevens in 1960 began to settle Worth down. He returned to Louisville in 1962 ready to prepare himself further for his role as the future chief of a media empire.[32]

Barry Jr., too, graduated from Harvard and went into broadcasting, working briefly at CBS and then NBC. His career was just beginning to soar there when his father called him home, saying it was time to join the family business. Unhappily, Barry Jr. returned to Louisville. Worth became assistant to the publisher of the newspapers and Barry Jr. was named assistant to the president of the WHAS television and radio stations as well as vice president of Standard Gravure.[33]

Sallie, a promising fiction writer, married and produced the first Bingham grandchild. Her first novel did not do well, but she experienced some success writing magazine pieces. There was a divorce and a second marriage and two more children, and more books that were not well-received.

Jonathan's death at age 21 in an electrical accident in 1964 stunned the family. Two years later, Worth was poised to become publisher when he, too, was stricken down in an accident while on vacation in Nantucket.

Only 32 and unprepared for the role, Barry Jr. saw his duty and stepped in to take his brother's place. Neither Sallie nor Eleanor, who was only 20 at the time, had demonstrated interest in joining family business – perhaps reflecting the understanding that their parents favored sons, not daughters, in the family enterprises.[34]

Barry Jr. was named assistant to the publisher at *The Courier-Journal* and *Times*. On his father's retirement five years later, Barry Jr. was awarded the titles of editor and publisher. Barry Sr. became chairman of the board, retaining controlling ownership of company stock.[35]

Under Barry Jr., the newspapers won five of the eight Pulitzer Prizes they would garner during the family's tenure, and Barry Jr. earned recognition for setting new standards for newspaper ethics. But the years were riddled with problems. Barry Jr. did not get along with the management team he had inherited, and, like his parents and sisters, he lacked basic financial knowledge.[36]

Beginning in the mid-1970s, the newspapers began a long period of economic decline. To make matters worse, Sallie and Eleanor returned home to Louisville in the late 1970s. They were added to the Bingham companies' board of directors and their father encouraged them both to become more active. Each owned about 4 percent of the voting stock in the companies and each stood receive another 7 percent when their parents died.[37]

But neither Sallie nor Eleanor were prepared for membership on a business board and their comments and demands were often an embarrassment to Barry Jr.[38] When Barry Jr. was forced to cut expenses, Sallie objected. "She had little knowledge of what actually went into the production of a first-class newspaper, but she saw her brother's efforts to slash costs as a betrayal of family traditions," say Tifft and Jones. "The fact that cutbacks were necessary at all was just another indication of his congenital incompetence, she felt."[39] Meanwhile, Sallie and Eleanor were largely dependent on company dividends for their living.[40]

Family members' inability to communicate effectively with one another was almost legendary. Sometimes they wrote letters to the editor of *The Courier-Journal* to express themselves on issues better left in the family.

Barry Jr. supported a number of attempts to get the family business on a right footing, but it was just too late. Sallie and Eleanor refused to sign a buy-back agreement that would have protected company stock from buyers outside the family. Barry Jr. pressed for putting competent outsiders on the board of directors but was rebuffed. According to Tifft and Jones, Eleanor, in particular, worried that outsiders would not understand that the $300,000 in dividends that she received annually "was a necessity, not a luxury."[41] Barry Jr. urged the family to hire a highly regarded family business consultant, but the family would have none of it.

Finally yielding to their son's wishes to get his sisters off the board, Barry Sr. and Mary voted to remove all the Bingham women from the board.[42] Sallie soon after offered to sell her stock to the family but made it clear that unless she was offered a price she thought fair, she would sell her shares outside the family.

There followed more years of infighting, accusations, misunderstandings, scapegoating and embarrassing publicity, until Barry Sr., with his wife's backing, decided to sell. Barry Jr. took the decision personally. "I looked at it as an active rejection of my leadership," he said.[43]

Barry Sr. was just a few weeks short of his 80th birthday in 1986 and still had ownership and voting control when the companies were sold. The Bingham empire fetched $448 million. Barry Jr., Eleanor, Sallie, and Worth's family became enormously wealthy in a sea of unhappiness, anger, and heartbreak. Barry Sr. passed away two years later.

Unlike Barry and Mary Bingham, Arthur and Iphigene Sulzberger, did not have a marriage made in heaven. Arthur's affairs were an open secret, and Iphigene turned a blind eye to his transgressions. "Paramount in Iphigene's mind was her duty to preserve the dynasty her father had built," say Tifft and Jones.[44]

Still, family unity was dear to both Arthur and Iphigene, and Iphigene, in particular, inculcated a sense of "all for one and one for all" among her four children.[45]

As the only son, Punch was destined as the successor to his father. His three future equal ownership partners, however, established their own successes. Marian became the first woman board member of the Ford Motor Company. Ruth trained as a journalist and was eventually named publisher and later chairman of the family-held *Chattanooga Times*. Judy became a physician.

Punch lived up to the faith that his mother and sisters had placed in him. He instituted budgets for the first time and remade the *Times* into a modern business.[46] He took the company public in 1969, careful to maintain voting control in the family. He began to diversify, and by 1978, the company had 37 subsidiaries.[47] He demonstrated his courage and won new accolades for the *Times* when he gave the go-head in 1971 to publish the top-secret study of US involvement in Vietnam known as the Pentagon Papers – despite company lawyers' warnings that the paper could be sued and ruined financially.[48]

After Arthur Sulzberger's death in 1968, Iphigene came into full bloom as the family's leader and as Punch's confidante in running the company – he was said to almost never make a major decision without consulting her.[49] She made each of the 13 cousins in the fourth generation feel special. Say Tifft and Jones: "Without words, without hugs, she communicated an intense interest in them and their welfare."[50] She also imbued them with the sense that the family and *The New York Times* were intertwined.

Unlike the beleaguered Barry Bingham Jr., Punch Sulzberger enjoyed the full backing of his family. As Tifft and Jones put it: "Whether the issue was the publication of the Pentagon Papers or jobs for their children at the

Times, Punch's sisters had given him their unwavering support, and he was careful never to abuse their trust."[51]

In 1986, the fourth-generation cousins came together with their parents in an astonishing show of commitment when all signed an agreement promising never to sell the company's Class B voting stock to buyers outside the family.[52] The agreement represented a financial sacrifice estimated at hundreds of millions of dollars for each of the family's four branches.[53] The show of solidarity would help fend off takeover attempts and assure family control should there ever be disaffection among family members. The Sulzbergers had learned well from the bitter Bingham family collapse just months earlier.

It would be inaccurate to suggest that everything went smoothly with the Sulzbergers. Arthur Hays Sulzberger, at age 41, suffered a coronary occlusion and for the rest of his life, could not bear weight in his left hand. Divorce or death afflicted the marriages of all the Sulzberger siblings. And, like his father and grandfather, Punch had the habit of hiring relatives. On a number of occasions, he had to ease out some of his father's family hires and some of his own.

The Bingham siblings, it appears, hadn't a whisper of a chance of becoming an effective team. Animosities in childhood were not addressed and perhaps not even recognized by their parents. Had they been, the family could have worked on Lesson 21, developing the Communication Skills so badly needed. The siblings would also have done well to develop a Family Code – their treatment of one another was often abysmal.

This is a family that surely could have benefited from Lesson 19, Next Generation Early Education. In this case, Mary and Barry Bingham missed the opportunity of teaching their children, particularly their daughters, about the responsibilities of ownership. As a result, Eleanor and Sallie were not adequately prepared for roles on the board. Instead, they exhibited a sense of entitlement – to the dividends they received and to their board seats.

The Binghams most surely had not learned Lesson 12, Graceful Pruning. When Sallie first showed her discontent and sought to sell her shares back to the family, the Binghams would have been wise to find a way to accommodate her. Ultimately, because the family could not come terms with Sallie, the family fell apart and the Bingham enterprises went out of the family.

Fortunately for the Sulzbergers, Graceful Pruning was not needed in the harmonious sibling generation. Had it been too bad, Adolph Ochs's will would have prevented any sibling selling shares until after Iphigene's death. That would have been a long wait – Iphigene lived to be 97.

The Sulzbergers practiced many of the lessons of Stage II. The children were educated about their responsibilities to the business and were encouraged to function as a team. Perhaps the lesson the family adopted most eagerly was Legacy of Values. The family's values were passed down from Adolph Ochs to Iphigene and Arthur Sulzberger and then to their children and their children's children. And throughout the generations, those values have passed back and forth between family and business.

Another lesson manifested powerfully in the Ochs-Sulzberger family is Successor to "Mom" – the family leader. In the first generation, Adolph Ochs played this role. After his death, his nephew Julius took up aspects of the role. Eventually, Iphigene became family leader and a very strong one. On her death in 1990, the mantle fell to Punch and his sister, Ruth.[54]

6 Stage III: The Cousin Collaboration

After a generation as a sibling partnership, a family business usually passes on to a larger group of cousins, entering the cousin-collaboration stage of evolution. A cousin-collaborative business can be owned exclusively by family members, or it may have non-family shareholders or even be listed on the public markets.

Just as the issues and challenges of the sibling partnership stage were different from the issues and challenges facing the owner-managed stage, so do the issues and challenges of Stage III, the Cousin Collaboration, differ dramatically from those of the Sibling Partnership.

Stage III becomes a balancing act. The family is much larger and ownership of the business is much more dispersed. There are probably more family shareholders who don't work in the business than who do work in it, and many family members are likely to live in distant communities. Not only are many geographically remote but they are, by now, also farther removed emotionally from the business's early origins and founding spirit.

The most critical issue now, from a family perspective, is the family's ability to offer its members sufficient freedom while at the same time winning their commitment to the business and building cohesion as a family. On the one hand, family shareholders need to know they are at liberty to liquidate their shares and exit ownership without being "ex-communicated" from the family. On the other, the business desperately needs family members to stay on as shareholders. If all the owners not active in the business decide to redeem their shares, the business could face a severe financial crisis. Far worse, however, is for the cousins to be locked into ownership legally, contractually, or emotionally. Wise families resist the temptation to force family members to be owners by tying shares up in trusts over which they have no control, adopting rigid shareholder agreements, or treating liquidation as a disgrace. Ideally, you want family members to feel they have the freedom to exit without judgment but to choose to identify with and stay a part of ownership in a business they believe in and like. The better a business-owning family can accomplish that balance at the cousin stage, the longer it will last.

From a business perspective, the most critical issue in Stage III is one of cultural and strategic adaptability. Held onto too tightly, traditions start to constrain action needed by a business in a changing world. While it won't want to throw out all of its traditions, the family aiming for long-term success will find that it has to amend some of its traditions and adapt them to assure the continued success of the business.

Again, the values that work in the Cousin Collaboration are different from the values that work in the Sibling Partnership – just as the values that are effective in the sibling stage differ from those that lead to success in the owner-managed stage. Where siblings relied on collectivism and mutual dependence, the cousins must turn to voluntary association – that is, commitment to the business that is freely chosen. In the sibling stage, equality of the brothers and sisters was a goal. Every effort was made to provide for the siblings equally, to offer each an equal inheritance, and to give each an equal vote. In Stage III, however, the cousins must learn to accept the fact that equality is no longer possible. If one of the siblings had just one child and another had five, there is almost no way the cousins can hold equal amounts of stock. The Stage III cousins will live in different towns and go to different schools. One may become a school teacher; another, a surgeon. Still another, if she is qualified, may join the business.

The willingness to share sensitive, personal information that was so important to the sibling generation is much less necessary to the cousin stage. What becomes critical now, as you will see in some of the lessons below, is that the cousins believe the business has a social purpose or a special family meaning. They need that second P that we talked about earlier – a Sense of Purpose that gives them the motivation to continue as part of a committed business-owning family. The decision to be a minority, non-employed family business owner is in many respects an irrational decision, particularly when family members could liquidate their stock and invest it elsewhere with more diversification – certainly with more liquidity. But when they see that the business has an intangible value, they see a reason to hold onto their stock and to make the sacrifices that business ownership requires, from learning about the business to traveling sometimes long distances to attend shareholder meetings.

In a letter to her nieces and nephews, Raya Strauss-Bendror, a second-generation partner in Strauss-Elite Ltd., an Israeli diversified food business, wrote: "Your mission is more difficult than our parents' and ours. So far, experience has shown that members of the first and second generations succeed in preserving the togetherness. But members of the third generation who have succeeded in doing so are few. And therefore, more will be demanded of you: more decision, more determination, more love and more faith." But she also added: "I believe in you. I believe that you will achieve the impossible."[1]

By Stage III, family businesses destined to endure have implemented, as appropriate, the lessons covered in the two previous chapters. If not, the cousins now take corrective action, instituting them as quickly as possible while at the same time moving on to address the following lessons, which are essential to Stage III.

LESSONS LEARNED

Essential from a Business Perspective

Lesson 27   Tradition of Change; Flexible Culture

If it is job of the sibling generation to lead a strategic and organizational renewal, it is the responsibility of the cousins in the third stage to expand on that accomplishment and reshape the company culture into one that is flexible and that embraces and encourages continuous adaptation and change. By doing so, the cousin generation ensures that the company is attuned to the need for frequent strategic renewal and is prepared to plan for change and implement it.

At Stage III, a family business is larger and more complex. It may, in fact, comprise several businesses or several product lines. Different parts of the enterprise will be coming into and going out of favor at different times. While it's desirable to retain some of the richness that characterized the first two generations of the family business, it is now also necessary for the family to see itself as being in a business that is flexible. While the company Grandpa founded started out making widgets, today the family may need to be comfortable with manufacturing metal parts. Perhaps it should entertain the notion of subcontracting some of the work instead of doing all the manufacturing itself. Next year, perhaps it will start using plastic instead of metal. In the cousin generation and beyond, the culture has to become one that is based on philosophies and values, instead of "That's the way we do things around here." And, the culture itself must stand for change.

If you're a member of the cousin generation, it's important that you not think just in terms of how Granddad did things or how Aunt and Uncle did things. That will hinder your ability to see things differently or to make needed modifications. It's not necessary to discredit your forebears in order to make changes. Instead, you can convey to the family and to the people in the business that your predecessors' greatest contribution was that they changed things in order to become successful entrepreneurs. They broke the mold or they challenged conventional wisdom or they did things that others told them couldn't be done. You want to inculcate the idea that the real culture of the past was not built around a set way of doing things but on a willingness to be innovative and to take risks.

Khalid Kanoo describes Y.B.A. Kanoo Group as an "evolving entity" and says, "It was a family decision to be flexible in our forward planning. We have annual business plans and long-range goals, but these are amended as current conditions dictate. We live in volatile times and so must respond to change in order to stay ahead."[2] What started out as a modest food trading business was turned into a shipping agency and importer. As the twentieth century progressed, it would accommodate itself to and capitalize on the introduction and growth of aviation and air travel, the discovery and development of oil in the region, striking technological change in the form of computers and communications systems, and enormous political and economic change. It followed a strategy of diversifying locally into different businesses and investing in many countries to avoid dependence on any one industry or nation and to make the family's future more secure.

"As history has proved to us," says Khalid Kanoo, "we cannot expect to remain in the same markets for ever [sic] because change will take place. If we don't change to meet the future, the future will change us."[3]

The family has also embraced change in terms of who is welcome and can advance in the business. Women family members have been in the company since the fourth generation, some of them overseeing operating divisions. The family, writes Khalid Kanoo, recognizes "the possibility that one day, a talented and ambitious Kanoo woman may seek appointment to the Board. ... [As] a part of our corporate evolution, that time will surely come."[4]

S.C. Johnson & Company started out in the 1880s as a parquet floor company before turning to floor wax. The second-generation leader started a Canadian subsidiary, established a 40-hour workweek for company employees, and launched many new products for cleaning, preserving, and other uses. The third-generation CEO created subsidiaries in France and Brazil and added still more products. The founder's great-grandson and namesake, Samuel Curtis (Sam) Johnson, diversified the product line even further, expanded the company into 45 countries, and extended the family into other interests, including financial services and outdoor recreational products. The Johnson enterprises are now in the hands of the fifth generation.

"Not only is it important that the next generation bring something new to the enterprise, it is equally important that they feel the great satisfaction that results from contributing a new dimension to the business," says Sam Johnson.[5]

Like S.C. Johnson and Kanoo, other long-lasting businesses expect each generation to bring change because they know adaptation and innovation are essential to long-term success.

Lesson 28   Spirit of Enterprise

The wisest business-owning families exemplify what I view as a "spirit of enterprise." They are open and flexible about the very definition of their business. Instead of saying they're in the business of making typewriters or mimeograph machines, they say, "We're in the business of business." This enables them, by the third stage, to be open-minded and relatively objective about the possibility that they may have to close down the company's first plant or drop the original product because it doesn't make sense anymore. And, they can do so without feeling that they've lost their core or their identity or their strategy. They simply move on to what does make sense, redefining the business, as appropriate, over time.

To succeed through time, great numbers of enduring business families move out of their original endeavor. The Henkel Group, based in Düsseldorf, Germany, was launched in 1876 as a small producer of household detergents; by 1999, however, detergents represented only 23 percent of the sales of this international family controlled conglomerate. Other sectors included chemical products, adhesives, and cosmetics.[6] Paksoy Tic San A.S., the Turkish company mentioned earlier, started out as a cotton-ginning enterprise; today it turns out margarine, oil, and soap.[7] LEGO Group, in Denmark, began as a carpentry company building homes, but it quickly changed course because of the Great Depression and made its mark as a toymaker.[8]

In keeping with the previous lesson, Tradition of Change, long-lasting, successful business families do not lock themselves into defining their business as the business of origin. Instead, they maintain the entrepreneurial spirit that characterized the founding generation. In 1927, J. Willard and Alice Marriott opened the nine-seat root beer stand that later became their first Hot Shoppe restaurant, in Washington, D.C. The Hot Shoppes chain grew to more than 100 restaurants, but in the late 1980s, Marriott management decided to phase out the fastfood eateries. In a warm, memory-filled ceremony, the founders' sons, Richard E. Marriott and J.W. Marriott Jr., both then in their sixties, oversaw the closing of the last Hot Shoppe in December 1999. J.W. Marriott Jr. recalled how his brother and he grew up in the restaurants. "All we ever talked about was the Hot Shoppes. It was our life," he said.[9]

But the owners understood very early that confining themselves to the original business would limit their thinking. The Hot Shoppes served as a launching pad for the family's institutional food services and catering operations, and just 10 years after the first restaurant opened, their company was providing in-flight meal service to the airline industry.[10] Today, Marriott International, with around $20 billion in annual sales, manages hotels, and resorts around the world, and Host Marriott Corporation has some $8 billion in assets, including more than 120 hotels.

When families see themselves as not being in the business that Granddad founded but in the business of business, they are more free to grow and adapt the company, to add or acquire other enterprises, and to sell or close the business of origin when it's no longer the appropriate venture to be in. And while they may not perpetuate the very business Granddad started, they can perpetuate the values that their grandfather may have had: the desire to see businesses grow and prosper and contribute to society; to create good places to work; and to provide family members with great life experiences and challenging professional opportunities and responsibilities.

When a family identifies itself as "a family that pursues enterprise," enterprise can apply to more than the business. It can also mean enterprise in family philanthropy or in encouraging family members or others to start other ventures.

Essentially, the spirit of enterprise promotes the idea that families can be purposeful and that they can work together to accomplish great things. Again, the Marriotts stand as an example. In 1989, they created the Marriott Foundation for People with Disabilities, to enhance employment opportunities for youth with disabilities. Under the foundation's banner, the family launched a program that has placed 6,000 young people with disabilities in competitive jobs.[11]

At some point in their history, families have to leave their business of origin. And when they can recast themselves as an "enterprising family," and not the "widget family," it invigorates them and frees them to think in ways that are bigger, broader, more creative, and more flexible.

As nostalgic as they were, the Marriott brothers had no need to feel disloyal to their parents or guilty when they closed the last Hot Shoppe. They used the occasion to announce that the Hot Shoppe name would be kept alive by renaming one of the restaurants in a Marriott hotel that stands on the site of one of the original Hot Shoppes. In so doing, they were honoring the past without being held back by it.

Lesson 29   Creative Capital

Eventually – often by Stage III, but sometimes earlier – family businesses have to think about new ways to come up with capital. By the time a business gets older and larger and the family gets older and larger, a number of things become inevitable: First, even with excellent estate planning, in most countries the family will have to face death taxes. Second, the business will have to transform, and capital will have to be invested or re-invested to enable it to grow, start new endeavors, or acquire other enterprises. Finally, it is also very likely that one or more family members will need to be bought out. All of these events call for substantial amounts of money. The family somehow has to find sources of capital that it hasn't so far needed to find.

A variety of options are open to them: going public, borrowing more money from the bank than they're used to, taking on equity or joint-venture partners, or selling part of the business. Very few business-owning families are comfortable with these choices. In many different words, what they are saying is, "Those are anti-cultural to us. We grew up in this business. We're going to stay private and we're not going to have a lot of debt. We don't want partners." Nevertheless, they know they have to be able to raise capital.

What I find is that long-lasting, successful family businesses approach this need in one of two ways or a combination of both. In one, they bite the bullet and change their financing paradigm. That is, they stretch their comfort zones and adjust their cultures to explore and implement some of the options we've just described. Or, second, they adopt a new business strategy, one that is less capital or investment intensive.

If your business requires large sums of capital to build new facilities, for example, your new strategy might be to shift from constructing plants or buildings to operating facilities that other people own. In other words, some families find ways to grow their businesses that don't require the same percentage of capital-to-growth that was required in the past. This might mean shifting a business from manufacturing to service. In the vending industry, for example, family business owners have turned to providing the sandwiches and other food items that go into vending machines rather than owning the equipment themselves, or they have started to provide food service in other ways, such as through mini-cafeterias that don't require expensive machines. Families in the funeral home business have turned from being owners to being funeral home operators as their businesses have been bought up in roll ups by larger companies.

Some business owners worry that by creating less capital – intensive ways to do business – by becoming operators rather than facility owners, for example – they may be opening themselves to competition by lowering the barriers to entry. I would argue, however, that when others get into your field because it takes less money, that doesn't mean they'll be good at it. Family businesses are often very good operators because they're good with people, they have strong cultures, and they have accumulated decades of unmatchable experience.

Farsighted, successful businesses families know that some day, they are going to need more capital than they have had access to through their traditional sources. They face up to that fact and move creatively to either adapt the business itself or they adapt their attitudes in ways that allow them to choose new paths for gaining access to funding. In 1985, nearly 100 years after it was founded, the Henkel family business, in Germany, went public in order to meet the needs of the growing business and family. In the 1990s, the family determined that future growth would have to be funded through such means as holding minority shares in other companies, spinning off strategic business units, or initial public offerings of subsidiaries.[12] By 2002, the company employed more than 46,000 people in more than 75 countries and anticipated annual sales of nearly €10 billion.

Lesson 30   Flexible Dividend Policies

Eventually, most family businesses pay dividends, particularly when there are family members who are owners but who are not involved in the management of the business. What often happens is that annual dividends are set at fixed amounts – $2 a share, perhaps, or $50,000 per shareholder. Over time, the amount is increased – to $3 a share, or $70,000 or $80,000 per shareholder. As a result, shareholders see dividends as a fixed amount of money, or an amount of money that is not tied to any rationale. They also come to expect dividends and to depend on them (and on the business) as part of their standard of living.

The most successful business-owning families, however, recognize that dividends need to be thought of as variable. That is, distributions need to reflect the business's real ability to pay and should be tied to profits. Then, when profits go up, dividends go up, but when profits go down, dividends go down. When dividends are variable, shareholders come to understand that dividends are a function of the company's success.

Variable dividends are important to responsible ownership. They encourage owners to say, "I really care about how the business is doing from a profitability point of view because it affects the money I get."

In addition, management can predict better how much money it needs to put aside for dividends because it will be using a set formula, such as 20 percent of profits. When profits go up, dividends go up by a constant percentage.

When dividends are based on profit, it takes some of the heat off management because management does not have to think about recommending dividends based on interpersonal or subjective considerations ("Lindsey's getting married. She'll need more money." Or, "Lionel's got a seriously ill child. Shouldn't we be helping him out?").

Savvy business families also take a real-world approach to dividends. They know that family members do expect dividends and, to some extent, rely on them. To allow for this bit of human nature, they stipulate that there will be a base dividend for each (equal) shareholder – for example, $50,000 a year. Even if the company has an off year, shareholders will each get $25,000. If the company is profitable, they may get more, depending on a variable formula.

Having a minimum dividend does more than make some family members happy. It also makes it clear to management that the business has to achieve a certain level of performance so that shareholders will receive their minimum return. It creates a source of discipline for management.

A flexible dividend policy requires some education at family meetings, so that shareholders understand the issues and support the philosophy behind the policy. They need to be clear on how dividends work, where dividends come from, and how paying dividends can sometimes inhibit the growth of the company by depriving it of needed cash.

Lesson 31   Infinite Time Horizon

We often say that family businesses have the advantage of being able to look at the long term, but nobody believes that more than families involved in really, really long-lasting businesses. They set their sights at infinity. Not only do they say, "This business will last forever," they also say, "I will never be the last generation, and my children will not be the last generation, and their children will not be the last generation of owners of this enterprise."

When, as owners, you commit yourselves to an infinite time horizon, you reinforce the notion of stewardship described in "Social Entrepreneur," Lesson #1 – the dedication to building an institution that can sustain itself well beyond its present leadership. Such a long view also helps you look at estate planning differently, encouraging you to think not in terms of solving your own generation's problems but of solving future generations' problems.

With respect to the business, you never consider making decisions that posture the business for intermediate-term benefit, let alone short-term gain. Instead, you're always positioning the business and investing for the long, long term. Consider the brand name of a company. Investing in identity and reputation has huge value that you can't calculate financially if you have an infinite time frame.

The renowned French company, Hermès SA, was founded in 1837 by Thierry Hermès, who produced custom-made saddles for European noblemen. Ever since, the company has been known for the quality and elegance of its products, which include silk goods, ready-to-wear clothing, watches, and perfumes. Hermès is now past 165 years old, but the family is still committed to keeping it a family controlled firm. Perhaps the fifth-generation leader put it best. Reflecting an attitude of stewardship, he said, "You are more proud thinking that the fruit of your labors will be harvested by your grandchildren."[13]

When families with an infinite view make business or investment decisions, they often understand that their decisions may not make a big financial difference 10 or 15 years from now. What they are saying, however, is "If it increases the inherent survivability, longevity, continuity, and strength of the business 15 years from now, it's a good thing to do." Having an infinite time horizon leads to a whole different way of thinking.

Lesson 32   Fair, Facilitated Redemption Freedom

In the cousin stage, the family formalizes and implements a process that allows family shareholders to redeem some or all of their ownership. This lesson bears some relationship to Lesson 12, Graceful Pruning, but is not quite the same. In Graceful Pruning, second-stage siblings are permitted or even encouraged, without stigma, to stay out of the business or to leave it if they are not interested in being a part of it. They exit the business altogether and are compensated for giving up ownership or the opportunity of ownership. They are still seen as a vital part of the family and, in that respect, Graceful Pruning addresses the interpersonal emotional issue of a sibling not being a part of the business.

Fair, Facilitated Redemption Freedom addresses the realities of a larger family and is more concerned with fair process. Recognizing that over time some shareholders will want to get out of ownership, partially or in full, the wise family draws up a policy that sets forth the terms and conditions and rules under which family members can redeem shares. The policy assures that a price is established fairly and family members understand that the rules apply to all. The procedure is "facilitated" in the sense that family members are welcome to the opportunity to redeem some shares.

An interesting model for this lesson is provided by Codorníu Group, where transparency and balance are emphasized. While selling shares outside the Raventós family is forbidden, a family member can sell shares to another branch of the family or to a holding company set up for the purpose of buying shares. The family sets the share price once a year so that every member knows what the price is. As part of a system of checks and balances to make sure that no one individual or branch becomes too powerful, the family has a rule that no shareholder may own more than 10 percent of Codorníu. Care is taken to see to it that there is an equilibrium of power among the branches. When one branch is seen as weaker than the others, for example, it is given preference for buying shares when they become available. If it does not do so, the holding company buys the shares.[14] Other business-owning families turn to the public market to resolve the redemption issue. Hermés went public in 1993 but retained 80 percent of the equity within the family. The public flotation reduced family tensions because it gave family members the ability to sell their shares without arguments over valuation, since share price was established by the fluctuating marketplace, not the family.[15]

This lesson is an excellent example of the first P, Policies Before the Need. The ability to redeem shares and to receive a fair price for them is a touchy issue in a family business. When a family develops a good redemption policy, people know what to expect and know they'll be treated fairly. Having such knowledge typically relieves family members of anxiety over personal security and freedom and actually strengthens their resolve to stay invested in the family's business. Paradoxically, the easier it is to sell, the less the desire to sell.

Lesson 33   Impersonal Ownership

This idea ties rather neatly to Lesson 31, "Infinite Time Horizon," and, to some extent, the notion of stewardship explored in Lesson 1, "Social Entrepreneur." What it suggests is that, even though you and other family members individually own stock in the business, you detach yourself from thinking of it as your personal, physical asset. You think of it, instead, as "vapor" or cloud-like – that is, as intangible and abstract, or as something that doesn't exist.

In some cultures, successful business families view the business as owned by the entire family and even by the future. In this framework, how many shares owned today by whom is an irrelevant concept. The family figures out ways, as a family, to take care of individual members' financial needs without reference to how much stock they own. Such families really prefer that members not think about how much stock they have and what they deserve because of what they own.

Laws and customs in some cultures, particularly in Asia and the Middle East, encourage this kind of thinking. In India, for example, individual family members often don't know how much stock they own because, to avoid death taxes, the shares have been put into so many people's hands, including family members, trustees, and many trusted friends of the family. Many in Europe put the ownership into a private foundation that the family, collectively, still controls.

Even in countries like the United States, where laws discourage such notions, some families have still found ways to practice impersonal ownership by putting their shares into 100-year dynasty trusts or offshore trusts or using some other means.

When a family adopts an attitude of impersonal ownership, people are less interested in redeeming shares because they don't feel like they own them. As a result, the business doesn't have to be so concerned about having to come up with cash to buy back stock. An impersonal-ownership perspective also helps the business focus on building long-term value rather than justifying its decisions by contemporary, Western, shareholder-value equations. People aren't saying, "The value of my shares didn't go up as much this year as they could have if I had been investing in Nokia." Instead, management is freed to concentrate on doing what's right for the distant future.

The downside is that, because it doesn't have to produce results quickly, the business might lack discipline. If the family is aware of this possibility, however, and sees to it that the business is run with professionalism, stewardship, good leadership, and good oversight (meaning a good board), then family members can trust that it is being run well and they don't have to be concerned about how much they own. What they own is the privilege of passing on the legacy to future generations.

Following a principle of impersonal ownership also benefits the family by increasing members' focus on the welfare of the total system. Family members ask, "What's best for the family?" or, "What's best for the business?" instead of, "What's in it for me?" It also increases the chance that they will see the business as an heirloom – something that's priceless and precious – which will make them less interested in selling.

In some ways, the concept of impersonal ownership is antithetical to Lesson 14, "Graceful Pruning," which emphasizes the advantages of facilitating stock redemptions. If you have a family that enthusiastically embraces impersonal ownership, however, you probably won't need to be concerned with making redemptions easier.

Essential from a Family Perspective

Lesson 34   Family Meetings

One of the key things that successful, long-lasting, business-owning families do to hold the family together is to have family meetings, typically from one to three times a year. Distinct from management meetings and shareholder meetings – which are centered on the business – family meetings focus on the interests of the family. Their purpose is to build the cohesion of the family and to enhance its sense of identity as a family. Family meetings are desirable long before Stage III, but by the third generation, they become essential. At a time when the family has grown larger and become dispersed and family members are increasingly remote from the business's origins, family meetings can instil a feeling of community and create a sense of family purpose.

Done properly, family meetings address many of the dimensions necessary to the continuity of the family: articulating the meaning and mission of the family; the education and personal development of younger members; the pleasurable and social aspects of being a family; and planning for the future. Family meetings can serve as a means of sharing experiences; acculturating new family members, such as in-laws; discussing the family's welfare; and sharing the joys and spirit of family philanthropy. Of crucial importance, family meetings should be fun. Almost nothing brings a family together as much as fun.

Family meetings encompass as many family members as possible, including young people. I find that successful families make family meetings as interesting and as easy to attend as possible in order to entice as many family members as they can. Often they're held in attractive settings where family members can enjoy any number of activities together – swimming, golf, hiking, and the like.

In larger families, the meetings are organized and run by the family council, a body elected by family members to oversee the affairs of the family as a family. In smaller families, the family itself operates as a council and plans the meetings.

Sometimes, families bring in outside speakers. Topics can cover almost anything, from communication skills to the family foundation. Family meetings can also include reports from committees of the family council.

As part of the "meaning and mission" function of family meetings, the family business can be placed on the agenda, too. Discussions can center on the history of the family business, the family employment policy, or how the family mission statement gets implemented in the business. Tours of the business or its facilities in different parts of the country can be included when a meeting is held in the headquarters town or in another community where plants or offices are located.

Whatever the agenda, planners should keep in mind that the real purpose of family meetings is to give family members a reason to be together and to be supportive of one another, and to share common interests together as a family. And if one of those interests includes being owners of a business together, fine. But the focus of family meetings should be on serving the interests of the family first, not the business.

Lesson 35   Education for Responsible Ownership

Successful business families take the rights and responsibilities of ownership very seriously. Because they do, they put substantial effort into educating family members about what it means to be a responsible owner. Often, education for ownership is included as a component of family meetings, or it may take place at shareholder meetings. Sometimes the business puts together the curriculum and resource people and hosts the sessions. Ownership education is aimed at not only current owners but also younger family members who will be future owners, and spouses of owners (who need to understand the realities that confront their husbands and wives), as well as beneficial owners if the shares are held in a trust.

In this educational process, family members explore what being a good owner entails. Through discussions, they come to understand what family members, as owners, can contribute to the business and how they serve as cultural ambassadors from the family to the business (see Lesson 36). They learn how to read financial statements and examine the role of private property in society. They discuss and debate the roles, rights, responsibilities and privileges of ownership, and look at what the concept of stewardship means. They discuss protocol (for example, can an owner call a manager directly or should she go through the board?). Sometimes, they even draw up a pledge or a covenant that sets forth their shared perspective as owners and an agreed-upon philosophy of what good ownership means to them – somewhat like the following:

The Owners' Pledge

——We pledge to treat one another with utmost respect.
——We will be open and honest in our interactions
    with one another.
——We will put the welfare of the company and of
    the family ahead of our own.
——We will speak with one voice.
——We will educate ourselves to perform our duties
    to the best of our ability.

———We will strive to be independent of the family
business for our financial support so as not to
harm the business out of personal need.

———We will work to earn the trust of all other
owners and extend our trust to them.

———We will communicate openly with one another.

———We will respect the role of management and the
role of the board.

———We will adequately prepare the next generation
for responsible and effective ownership.

Source: *Family Business Ownership: How to be an Effective Shareholder*, by Craig
E. Aronoff and John L. Ward, Family Enterprise Publishers, 2001.

Resource people in this education process might include an attorney talking about the duties and responsibilities of ownership; financial experts
who can teach accounting basics and help family members understand
financial statements; or family members versed in the history of the business's ownership and how it has been passed on. Other resource people can
include family or non-family executives who can share their insights on
how being an owner affects the business; family members who are on the
board or independent directors who can talk about family business governance, the shareholders' relationships with the board, and how the board
works; or family business consultants, who can cover the relationship of
ownership to the business.

The subject of responsible ownership offers rich opportunities for delib-
eration and discussion and, as successful families have found, such explo-
ration helps unite the family members in their commitment to the business
and its future.

Lesson 36   Active, Involved Ownership

There is a real difference between being a passive owner and an active
owner. A passive owner says, "I own shares in the business. I'll watch them
like I would watch any investment. I'll enjoy the financial rewards when
they come, but that's where my interest ends and my role stops."

An active, involved owner, however, says, "I have a real duty to be a good
owner and to take advantage of my role as owner to contribute value to the
business. The way I can do that is by being visible to the business – letting
management know that I'm interested, that I care, that I understand, and
that my decision to be an owner is an informed decision. I'm an owner by

choice, by enthusiasm, and by commitment. I'm an owner because I believe in the business and its potential."

This lesson really focuses on owners who are not working in the business, or who are employed in the business but at lower levels where they might not, in the course of their work, be fully knowledgeable about strategy or governance – aspects of the business they need to know as owners. Owners who work in the business but at higher levels are presumed to be active owners because of their involvement as managers.

When owners are passive, they are not visible to the business. Non-family managers and employees begin to ask questions among themselves: "I wonder how long these owners are going to be happy owners? Are they only interested in dividends? Do they fight among themselves? Do you think they're going to sell the business? Is it only a matter of time before we're out the door?"

Farsighted owners have learned, however, that active, involved owners are good for the business. They are committed to the business, they care about its values, and they are vigilant. It really strengthens good managers to know that owners are paying attention, because if owners are attentive and are informed, involved, and knowledgeable, their decisions in support of management are more solid and durable and managers in turn can put more faith in the owners. As a result, management gains the confidence to take risks, implement strategy, and make decisions.

Being an involved owner is quite different from being an owner who looks over the shoulders of managers and second-guesses them. That kind of oversight has managers saying, "I wonder if I should be careful. Maybe I should be more conservative. I wonder if the owners are going to disagree with this decision. I wish I could get them out of my hair because all they're going to do is mess things up."

Active ownership encompasses three things:

1. *Being Knowledgeable About and Supportive of the Business Strategy.* When this is the case, management knows that ownership is behind it on the strategy and will stay faithful to it. But if something goes wrong with the strategy, the owners will see it sooner rather than later and will take corrective action, as owners, through the board of directors.

2. *Serving as a Cultural Ambassador to the Business on Behalf of the Family.* Involved owners constitute a proactive force in the culture of the business. They represent the values of the family. By living those values, they not only set an example for the business but they also convince those in the company that the family's values statement is more than mere words

on paper. They give it life by being visible in the business, attending ceremonies, upholding traditions, and making clear in a multitude of ways what it is the family stands for.

3. *Being Wise and Educated Governors.* Governance in a family business centers around the relationship between management, ownership, and the board. Owners elect the directors and determine the values, the vision, and the goals that will guide the board and management. Family business experience as well as research has demonstrated over and over again that companies with good governance perform better. Successful families realize that if owners understand and practice good governance, they will be a source of strength to the business.

Some families demonstrate their commitment to Active, Involved Ownership by stepping away from running the business and adopting a governing role. The family owners of the Murugappa Group, a conglomerate based in Chennai, India, are an example. After the premature deaths of two key family executives in 1996, the family decided that it was important to the future of Murugappa that it rely less on family members for day-to-day responsibility of the business units as managing directors. After much discussion, the Murugappa Group established a new governance structure in 1999. Family members withdrew from leadership of the individual business units, making way for professional managers, and assumed positions on a newly created Murugappa Corporate Board. The board includes five family members (two from the third generation and three from the fourth), three independent directors, and the Murugappa CFO.

Essentially, the Murugappa Group has moved from being family operated to family governed. The new structure enables family board members to concentrate on business strategy. The extended family has supported the process by developing a statement of Corporate Values and Beliefs, as well as a Bill of Rights and Responsibilities for Family Member Owners. Next up will be the development of a family constitution. While family members may still join the business, their development and training is now focused not on their becoming unit managing directors one day but upon rising to leadership at the governing level.[16]

Lesson 37   Nose In, Fingers Out

This is an expression that I have heard from many successful business-owning families. These wise families recognize and accept the limits of ownership. They know where ownership starts and stops, where the board starts and stops, and where management starts and stops. They realize, for example, that it's out of line for owners to ask the business for personal favors ("Can you send some employees over to help me move some furniture?" or a more subtle request to senior management for help with a personal charity). They understand that they should not be expressing opinions about a particular employee to management but that they should be going through proper channels, speaking first to the owners' representation on the board.

They are also vigilant about spouses and children who may sometimes exercise prerogatives as if they were owners, just because they're married to an owner or the child of one.

Many successful families use "nose in, fingers out" as a code statement for their role as owners. To them, it says, "Now let's remember! We can have our nose in there, but we've gotta keep our fingers out. That's management's job."

In other words, they don't overstep their boundaries as owners and cause problems for the business. They're informed, and they're involved, but they don't meddle.

Codorníu has set up a system to prevent family members from having access to managers and taking up their time. It wants its managers focused on making profits and so has established a department to resolve shareholders' problems.[17]

Lesson 38   Respect Managers and Managing

An important part of being an educated owner or family member is to truly believe and understand that managing a business is a very complex and demanding challenge. It requires talent that very few people possess. Successful business-owning families recognize this, and they have a profound respect for the array of skills that excellent managers bring to the task.

Such families know that managing means more than being "good with people" or sharing your opinion at meetings or understanding the customer's preference or being good at finance. It is all of these and more – having a gift for strategic thinking, exceptional leadership abilities, and diplomatic expertise all come to mind. It is art and craft and science all rolled into one, and it is enormously creative.

Nevertheless, unless family business owners are experienced or sophisticated enough to understand the demands of effective management, they often tend to regard management as less difficult than it is. They and their families may too easily cast their judgments on managers and be too sure that if only their child was in the manager's chair, he could do better.

Understanding the complexity of management is critical when a family is dealing with matters of succession and continuity of leadership of a business and considering which family members are eligible to participate at senior levels. When a family doesn't have a deep respect for the skill of managing, it tends to be far too casual about family members taking positions in the company and being promoted. As we have seen in Lesson 10, "Many Non-Family Executives," when a family does not set standards high enough for family members entering the business and being promoted, it dilutes management strength because the best managers become discouraged and leave, or they simply aren't attracted to the company in the first place.

Respect for managers and managing becomes especially critical by Stage III and beyond. A business that reaches the third or fourth generation, as noted earlier, is likely to be much larger and more complex than it was when the first and second generations ran it. In Stage III, a business has more cultural issues to deal with. It may be undergoing a strategic transformation. It will be faced with more sophisticated governance issues. It may be expanding internationally, and it will most likely need to be investing in more subtle areas, such as information technology, marketing, or the development of people.

It is very difficult to find outstanding managers who can lead the large, sophisticated businesses that we begin to find in Stage III. Business-owning families at this point more easily come to the conclusion that top managers – the CEO and other senior executives – need to come from outside the family. The larger the company, the more likely that will be the case. Again, the Henkel Group provides a good example. For three generations, the leaders of the company bore the Henkel name. In 1980, however, Konrad Henkel, then 65, became the last CEO from the family when he turned leadership over to a senior non-family executive. At the same time, a cousin ceded his position as executive manager.[18] Somewhat like the Murugappa Group, the Henkel family has redefined its role to become one of exercising responsible ownership and supporting non-family executives who run the company.

Lesson 39   Family Education

We've touched on the education of family members in the lessons on communications and ownership. In large, older, successful family businesses, however, education is often very broad, and it occurs in a variety of ways, formal and informal, sporadic and continuing.

I see education taking place in three major areas:

1. *Interpersonal Skills.* Successful families give a lot of time and attention to (1) educating the family as a family, so that it can function more effectively as a group, and (2) educating family members as individuals, so that they can each be more effective as a person.

To enhance the family's ability to work together and accomplish objectives together, families concentrate on mastering problem-solving and decision-making skills. They provide experiences to young people to help them develop organizational or managerial talents – for example, learning to run a good meeting or to be an effective meeting participant or a good committee chairman. Toward that end, younger family members might be asked to help plan the next family reunion.

Consensus building is another important group skill. Even if a family is too large to make decisions by consensus, it will have family committees or a family council or a business board of directors that will operate on a consensus model.

2. *Personal Growth and Development.* Some families enhance personal growth in a very big picture, visionary way. At the same time, they build cohesion by providing very special educational experiences that the family can enjoy together – experiences family members would not have the opportunity to have if they were not part of such a unique family and not involved in the family education process. They do this by inviting exceptionally distinguished speakers, world authorities even, to make presentations at their family meetings. Guest speakers might address such topics as how the shape of the economy is changing, how technology will affect people's lives, understanding and addressing poverty, or what's going on in politics, public education, physics, or the arts. The family might also bring in outstanding motivational or inspirational speakers.

If the family is large enough, it might also have educational sessions or activities that help younger family members make their way through life. Some families I know have a program where the young people who have recently attended college meet over a meal at a family retreat with the kids who are in high school. The older ones talk about their college experiences, how they prepared for campus life, what they did at school, what they would differently if they had the chance, and so on. Other families have young adults who are fairly new to the workforce talk to the family members who are still in college. The older ones describe what their first job was like or tell what they did to get it. I even know one family where young mothers and fathers talk about parenting with young couples who don't yet have children.

Personal development, then, can take many forms – from preparing young people for college or their first job to learning about the world at large.

3. *Family Culture.* It's wonderful to see how thoughtfully some families pass on the culture, values, and history of both the family and the business to the next generation. The grandparents in one family have formed a committee and run little programs for the younger children – kids from about 8 to 12 years old. The grandparents explain the family tree to them and show family pictures, getting the kids involved by asking questions like, "Which one of these is your great grandfather?" "Can you guess which one of these kids is your grandmother?" They tell stories about the family and its background.

Other families conduct sessions on the history of the family and the business for older children or, as already pointed out, for people new to the family, such as in-laws. And, as indicated earlier, successful business-owning families often seek out ways to show how the family's values and culture influence and enhance the business.

As these examples suggest, families are very inventive about the way they educate. As families get larger – 40, 50, 100 people – the very best create a council of elders or some other subset of the family that looks after the welfare of individual family members. They act as mentors or coaches, making sure that individuals' developmental needs get met. "Why doesn't one of us call young Juan and see how he's doing?" one might suggest. "He's going to college next year. Maybe we can connect him with somebody else in the family who graduated recently."

What sets these large, older family businesses apart in the way they approach education is their remarkable conscientiousness. They are deliberately attentive to family members as individuals and to the family as a group.

Lesson 40   Family Member Development Program

This lesson is an important extension of the personal growth and development aspect of the Family Education lesson. It begins when families realize that they want the next-generation family members in the business to be suited to it and effective in it. "We really want them to get some great background," such families say. Even more than providing their young people with good experience, they want to be sure that joining the business will be a good match for them, because they view suitability as necessary to success. "We want family members who can be successful in the business – for their sake as well as for the business's sake," they say. "We want our young people to have an opportunity to know themselves well enough that they can make a good career decision about whether or not to come into the business and what role they can play in it if they do."

In many families, these concerns lead to a program of career counseling, vocational aptitude testing, and coaching for young people who are considering careers in the family business. Often, families will bring in an outside consultant, such as an industrial psychology firm, to do the formal testing and assist with the process, beginning with young people in the 14 to 16 age bracket.

But in many cases, people in the family start to say, "What about family members who don't want to work in the family business? Shouldn't we offer these resources and these opportunities to them as well?" Not doing so, they argue, violate the family's principle of not favoring family members who work in the business but valuing just as much those family members who are interested in art or teaching or some other career. So the family makes a decision to offer vocational testing, career mentoring and other personal growth and development resources to all of its young people, regardless of their ultimate career destiny.

Soon, in some of these families, someone begins to ask, "Why shouldn't these resources be available to all family members, regardless of age? What about middle-aged or older people who would like some feedback about what their vocational preferences might be, or people who are interested in entering the world of work after being out for a while?" Before long, such families begin to offer resources and programs not just to teenagers and young adults but also to all family members, regardless of age.

Such resources may facilitate a young mother going back to work after the last child starts school, or encourage a middle-aged family member to return to college and get a degree. They may even convince some family members in the business that they would be happier elsewhere.

Ultimately, the smartest business families know their businesses will be more successful when they attract only the most suited family members. They also know that when family members outside the business are happy and fulfilled, they will in turn be more supportive of the business and less likely to find fulfillment only if they work for the business.

Lesson 41   Family Leadership Succession

Early in this book, we talked about the need for a "Successor to Mom," and how Mom was probably the unacknowledged leader of the family. By the third stage, successful businesses have found they have to be even more conscious of and deliberate about recognizing the importance of the family leadership role and seeing that it is filled.

In Stage III, the distinction between the business leader and the family leader is a very important one. The business leader guides the business and, in an equally critical role, family leader guides all of the family activities – family meetings, family education, acculturation of in-laws, a council of elders, family reunions, and the like.

Typically, the family leader and the business leader are not one and the same. Older successful business families have learned that when the business leader is also the family leader, the message that comes across is that the reason the family is doing what it is doing (having a reunion or a retreat, e.g.) is to support, strengthen, and protect the business. But that's not the point of family leadership. The family leader looks after all those things the family would do as a family whether or not its members owned a business together. The family would *want* to do an education program or engage in philanthropy as a group, whether or not it owned a business. It would *want* to have reunions. Members would want to have fun together and help each other. The family leader nurtures the spirit of the family and sees to it that the joys and issues of being a family are not swallowed up by the demanding concerns of the business.

Long-lasting business families pay as much attention to family leadership succession as they do to business leadership succession. "How do we identify that leader?" they ask. "How do we select that person? By a vote?" Although it is almost always an unremunerated, voluntary position, I know one business family that pays the family leader the same salary that the family CEO of the business receives. By doing so, the family is making a very important, symbolic point: "We value the person who leads the family every bit as much as we value the person who leads the business."

Most families would argue that the kinds of talents and skills you need to be a business leader are different from the competencies required of the family leader. People who run a family like they run their business may not be the best people to guide the family. Family leadership calls for a different touch, a different style, and a different perspective. The family leader needs to be seen as someone who is interested in every branch of the family, not just his or her own branch. Very often, a competent family leader is someone who has demonstrated very effective leadership skills in a volunteer organization.

By Stage III, the family leader is probably not Mom, and, again, is not necessarily a woman. Often, family leadership is not even relegated to an individual. It may be a group of older uncles or aunts who used to be in the business, or a council of elders. It may not even be direct descendants-in-laws who can sometimes be very effective in this role. It can be filled by older, wiser family members. But age doesn't matter. The family leadership role can be played by anyone who can bring cohesion and care to a large, sophisticated, complex organization.

The important thing is to understand how necessary the family side of things is to the ongoing success of a family firm, and to plan diligently for family leadership succession.

Lesson 42   Provide for Family Members "In Need"

From time to time, individuals in an extended family are going to have personal problems or special needs. These could be substance abuse, depression, health problems, or even legal troubles. There may be a family member with retardation or some other disability who requires life-long care arrangements of some kind. Or a family member may be experiencing financial difficulties and feel forced to sell his stock, even though he would prefer to stay an owner and even though the family has hoped he would stay an owner.

When someone is going through a hard time, the family needs to respond – whether it helps the troubled person find counseling or other resources or provides emotional or even financial support.

Thoughtful, farsighted, long-lasting business families anticipate that personal problems and special needs are going to arise. Instead of waiting for the inevitable to happen and deciding what to do in a crisis mode, they prepare by developing a philosophy about how such events or circumstances are going to be handled and they communicate the expectations throughout the family.

Families respond quite differently to the family-member-in-need issue. Some adopt a policy that responsibility for attending to problems lies with the beset individual's nuclear family. Others take the position that every adult in the family has to take personal responsibility for his or her own affairs and that the family is not going to bail people out or be the source of a solution to a problem.

Still others, particularly in Mediterranean and Eastern cultures, believe in the philosophy that it's the extended family's role and responsibility to help family members in need. Some of them even maintain a pool of cash that's used to help individual family members. Often overseen by a family council or council of elders, it might be used to assist someone in financial straits or to provide for a family member with a disability. Alternatively, it might be used to offer someone a special opportunity that he or she might not otherwise have – a college education for a brilliant young person whose parents died early, for example.

In the United States, business families are more likely to take the approach that a troubled individual's nuclear family has the responsibility of providing assistance. The immediate family might find a way to tide over a member mired in money problems so that he's not forced to sell his stock – perhaps by making it possible for him to borrow against his stock either from the family or from the company. Alternatively, if someone has a disability, other members of the nuclear family might contribute to a trust to take care of her.

Approaches vary among successful business families. The common threads, however, are that they understand that individuals will have problems, they discuss and adopt a philosophy of how problems will be dealt with, and they communicate that stance throughout the family so that everyone knows what to expect.

Lesson 43   Roles for All in Family Association

At this point in its evolution, the business is no longer the center of the universe. The family is much more the center, and the business is but one of its interests. In many of these Stage III lessons, we've talked about how the most successful business-owning families now take a position that they recognize, value, support and endorse family members who have interests other than being in the business. They deliberately discourage the dangerous presumption, so common to family businesses, that the most valuable people in the family are those who are working in the business. They see all family members as valuable, whether or not they're in the business.

The eight sons in the fourth generation of the Kanoo family inherited Y.B.A. Kanoo. However, one of them, Abdul Latif Kanoo, chose to work outside the family business, pursuing a career with the Bahrain government instead. Nevertheless, his family and he are part of the family system. As he puts it, "We are brothers, irrespective of whether I work with the company or not. We are a family."[19]

Long-lasting business families have learned that when a family becomes larger, it very consciously needs to find more opportunities for people to contribute and participate and lead – on the family side. When family members have meaningful roles to play, they become more interested in and committed to the family. Their involvement also reinforces the point that people who contribute to the long-term welfare of the family are every bit as important as the people who contribute to the long-term welfare of the business.

In addition to the top family leader, there are many opportunities for participation and leadership in a family. Large, successful business families commonly have a family council, and the council itself often has three or four or more committees and task forces that need effective leaders and participants. These might include a committee on family education (see Lesson 39), a task force that looks at how to prepare family members for board participation, a reunion planning committee, a committee that plans family meetings, or a family philanthropy committee (see Lesson 44).

At first, all four members of the fifth generation of the S.C. Johnson family chose to join the family business. Eventually, however, Winnie, one of Sam Johnson's daughters, decided not to seek a full-time management position in the business because she was living in another state and raising a family. However, she still plays an important role in the family and its endeavors – she is president of the Johnson Family Foundation and sits on the board of the Johnson Financial Group. In addition, she and her mother sit with the other four family members and three trusted advisors on a decision-making committee called the Family Business Council. One of its goals is identifying and nurturing promising members of the sixth generation who show interest in the family business.[20]

Very common but complex are committees on communication and information. They may put out the family newsletter, create the family web page, or help with the family reunion by organizing programs or activities that enable people to get to know each other better or be more informed. This committee can also determine what information should be coming from the business to the family and how to present it.

Some families have a committee that puts together a family archive or writes the family history, or a task force on succession planning in the business from the family perspective. In some families, next-generation development is overseen by a task force or a subcommittee of the education committee.

Family foundations and family offices, which look after the personal business affairs and philanthropic interests of large families, offer excellent opportunities for involving family members in leadership and service roles. At Murugappa, in India, custom precludes the sisters and wives in the family from working in the business, but they play leadership roles in the family's foundation.[21]

People can be involved directly in the day-to-day operations of a family office or serve on a committee that provides oversight. A foundation will have its own board, which will need the service of willing, able family members. I've known some families to set up a second foundation with a second purpose, as a means of providing more leadership opportunities for family members.

Smart business-owning families deliberately create meaningful roles that offer talented, giving, helpful family members who are not in the business a chance to shine. What's more, they treat the leaders on the family side – the family council members and the foundation directors, for example – with the same level of respect, appreciation, and admiration that they shower on family members who serve on the business's board or in its management.

Lesson 44   Family Philanthropy

In my experience, larger, older, more successful families develop an increasing interest in, sophistication about, and commitment to philanthropy. One reason is that more people in a family have an opportunity and an ability to participate in and contribute to philanthropy that have an opportunity to be involved in the business. Philanthropic interests typically touch a wider percentage of the family members than business interests do.

A second reason is that for many successful families, "giving back" is a fundamental part of the value system. They want to demonstrate appreciation for the privilege and abundance they have enjoyed. Becoming more actively involved in philanthropy as a family offers a meaningful way to do that.

Again, families approach philanthropy in different ways. Some provide education to family members so they can be more effective at philanthropy, enjoy it, and learn from one another's experiences. However, individual family members are encouraged to follow their own passion in their giving. Other families encourage and facilitate the development of foundations by branches of the family.

Others take it a step further. While still encouraging individual giving according to one's personal interests or the establishment of foundations by family branches, these families say, "What if we stood for something collectively as one large, extended family and pool monies from everyone or all the branches into one extended-family foundation?"

Some families may actually create an identity as a family around a certain interest area, such as the U.S. Kennedy family (a "political" family business!) and its association with the Special Olympics. Others select a small group of targeted interests. The Levi Strauss Foundation, for example, concentrates on communities around the world where Levi Strauss & Co. employees and contractors' employees live. It supports programs in three areas: preventing the spread of HIV/AIDS, increasing economic development opportunities, and ensuring access to an education.[22] Among the hundreds of grants the Levi Strauss Foundation has made in recent years are disbursements for programs to provide HIV/AIDS education in South Africa, Hong Kong, Korea and other countries; to support micro-enterprise development and training for economically disadvantaged people in Vietnam and the Philippines; and to provide scholarships or other educational assistance to young people in Hungary, Turkey and Cambodia.

In addition to the company foundation, there are now also five different foundations set up by family members. One, for example, is the Evelyn & Walter Haas, Jr. Fund, dedicated to philanthropy in the San Francisco Bay Area, where the company is headquartered. The late Walter A. Haas, Jr. was a Levi Strauss chairman and the great grandnephew of the company founder. The current chairman, Robert D. Haas, sits on the foundation's board of trustees with his siblings and mother.[23]

A foundation or some other form of collective philanthropy brings many strengths to a family. It creates more opportunities for family members to identify with the family, as well as to appreciate and acknowledge their good fortune. Individuals born into business families committed to philanthropy grow up knowing they are not only the great-grandchildren of the founder of a nationally known cookie company, for example, but also come from a family that's a leader in supporting cancer research or providing shelters for victims of domestic abuse. Families that actively engage in philanthropy also often find it easier to raise children who are less spoiled by wealth and who therefore have a better chance of being effective, responsible business owners.

Traditionally, families have set up charitable foundations that give money to many of the organizations in the communities where their businesses were founded. Today, more families are evolving away from community-based giving toward more strategically focused, issue-oriented philanthropy. They feel they can make more impact by centering their efforts on one or two carefully selected areas. This change is also a reflection of the fact that as they grow older and larger, families become less attached to the community of origin. The business may no longer be headquartered in the town in which it was founded, and a large percentage of the family may live elsewhere. Some families do both, however. A family may still view the community as "the source of our success," and even though its headquarters are no longer located there, it continues to support the local institutions. At the same time, it sets up a separate vehicle for engaging in philanthropy with a more strategic purpose.

Lesson 45   One Family

An epiphany of sorts takes place around the third or fourth generation of long-lived, successful business families. Until it occurs, a family most likely is experiencing the aftereffects of second-generation sibling rivalry. Brothers and sisters in the sibling stage typically harbor some unresolved negative feelings toward one another – a brother may be sure the parents favored his sister, or a sister may feel her brother got all the lucky breaks in the business. Even though they are owners together, they start to organize themselves into branches. "We're our own family," Sibling One says of himself, his wife, and their children. "We're our own family," echoes Sibling Two, referring to herself, her husband and their children. And so on.

Soon, their attitudes get passed on to the third generation: "Your Grandpa and Grandma thought your Uncle Harold walked on water. That's why he's running the company today." Or, "If it weren't for your Aunt Lorna and me, this company wouldn't make it. Your Uncle Steve has never pulled his weight." Or, "Our interests just aren't the same as theirs. Even though we're in business together, we don't have to do everything together."

The sibling generation often creates or magnifies the differences and distinctions among the branches, and when the third-generation cousins come along, the family is fragmented and uneasy. Very often, the members of the third generation are carrying on an inherited rivalry among themselves, with cousins they don't even know very well because they didn't grow up in the same house or even the same town.

Then one of the cousins or second cousins says, "Let's bury the hatchet." Wisely, the cousins realize their parents' or grandparents' rivalry doesn't have to be their own. They begin to understand that, as an ownership group, they need to be able to work well together. Some of them even begin to discover that they actually like one another – maybe they are closer to their second cousins than to their own brothers and sisters or first cousins. The cousins and second cousins may be closer in age to one another than they are to their siblings and may have more in common. Some of the cousins find they have fun together at family reunions or working on a committee together, and one will finally say to another, "You're a good guy, no matter what my mom and your dad said about each other."

Eventually, one of the cousins – or more typically, one of the second cousins – reflects on the animosity that grew out of the second generation and says, "You know, that was all kind of silly. We're all one family. Let's not make distinctions about which branch does this and which branch does that." In addition, the cousins learn to move forward again as one family.

When the branch philosophy lingers on, family members feel that each branch has to be represented on the business board, the family council, the family foundation, and committees. One branch does not trust another, or one fears that another will gain too much status or recognition.

I see the one-family concept most often in the older families of Europe and Asia. When it prevails, branch representation gives way to drawing on the most able people from the larger family as a whole. Decisions are based on one person-one vote, and no one worries that the branch with 14 members gets 10 more votes than the branch with four. There's a spirit of selecting people who will best serve the welfare of the whole family.

Arriving at a one-family concept is inevitable in successful families – the Rockefellers, who managed it in the fourth generation, come to mind. So do the Ochs-Sulzbergers, whose unification was endorsed and formalized by the cousins in the fourth generation. More about that later in this chapter.

There are many sad examples of families that could not forge themselves into one family. Mentioned earlier was Steinberg, Inc. After Mitzi Dobrin, a third-generation daughter, was forced out of Steinberg Inc. in 1985, she lost interest in being an owner of the company. In the simplest terms, she, her mother and sisters owned the controlling shares of Steinberg, but the shares were tied up in trusts and the sisters were all trustees of one another's trusts – an arrangement set up decades earlier by Sam Steinberg. It was meant to minimize taxes but Sam didn't take into account what might happen if his daughters began to disagree on how the trusts were managed. The sisters could not come together as a unified body of shareholders who put the good of the company ahead of their own interests. After four years of family feuding, the Steinberg empire was sold in 1989 to a corporate raider who began selling it off in bits and pieces.[24]

One of the grisliest tales of a failure to unite as one family belongs to the Guccis, of Italy. According to Sara Gay Forden's history of the family, the seeds of its destruction were sown in Stage I by Guccio Gucci, the founder of a small leather goods company in Florence in 1921. Three sons – Aldo, Vasco, and Rodolfo – worked in the business, and, Forden notes, Guccio "often played [them] off against each other, believing that competition would stimulate them to perform better."[25] When he died, Guccio left the company that bore his name equally to the sons.

Aldo became the "driving force" in the second generation, says Forden.[26] His three sons – Giorgio, Paolo, and Roberto – and Rodolfo's son, Maurizio, all joined the growing business. When Vasco died, Aldo and Maurizio became 50–50 shareholders in the core company, Guccio Gucci. Aldo, who gave each of his sons 3.3 shares, secretly felt that his brother's contribution did not equal his 50 percent ownership in Guccio Gucci, and he began to direct more profits into one of the family's other enterprises, Gucci Parfums SpA, where Rodolfo had a lesser stake.[27]

Friction developed as Paolo grew discontented at not having more of a say in the company. He also started to raise questions about its finances.[28] When Paolo initiated steps to start a business of his own, Aldo fired him. Fighting erupted between Aldo and Rodolfo as Rodolfo sought a larger stake in the profitable perfume business.

When Rodolfo died in 1983, Maurizio, inherited the 50 percent stake in the Gucci empire. The next year, he and his cousin Paolo made a secret pact – Maurizio would buy Paolo's shares and gain control of the company. The agreement fell apart, but not until after Maurizio became chairman and his uncle, Aldo, was effectively "neutralized."[29] Two years later, Aldo at age 81 went to prison for a year for U.S. tax evasion, a result of earlier whistle blowing by Paolo.[30]

Eventually, Maurizio joined forces with a financial partner, Investcorp, which obtained Paolo's small stake and finally succeeded in buying out Aldo and his other two sons. Maurizio was not up to the demands of running a company as complex as Gucci had become. In time, he found himself at war with his new partner and, in 1993, facing both personal and company bankruptcy, he sold his holdings to Investcorp. After 62 years, Gucci had fallen out of family hands. It was not the end of Maurizio's story, however. He was gunned down by a hit man in 1995, and three years later, his embittered ex-wife, Patrizia, and four accomplices were convicted of his murder.

The Gucci case is one of the more extreme examples of lack of family unity. Generally, unless the branches can come together and operate as one, the family and its business will partition. Two branches will buy out one branch, and then one of the remaining branches will buy out the other and the business will become small again. It's pruning by big branches, not by individual needs or preferences, and big-branch pruning puts a huge financial strain on the business. In addition, unfortunately, families that fracture in one generation tend to perpetuate fracturing in future generations. If a parent can't learn to work with a sibling, how can he teach his own children to work together?

Successful, long-lasting business families break this cycle because someone in the third or fourth generation – or better, sooner – is wise enough and brave enough to say, "Let's act as one family."

Lesson 46   Family's Mission Statement is Central

Many of the lessons you've read so far suggest that the good of the business comes first – family members should be professional, they should respect managers and managing, they should prepare themselves if they want to join the business, the family should operate on a principle of merit, and so on.

Yet, in one of the many paradoxes that make up family business, the lesson here is that when the family puts together its family mission statement, the family has to come first. For two reasons.

First, in Stage III, you are trying to keep an extended family together as a group of owners. In order to maintain people's interest and involvement in the business, they need to perceive a family purpose behind it. Although they may recognize the business as an heirloom, a legacy, or a cultural statement, most family members in the third or fourth generation do not work in the company and are not interested in it as a business. They have to see that holding on to the company and giving it attention and sacrifice are in the best interests of the family.

The second reason the family comes first is that it needs a sense of cohesion and a feeling of pride that will make people want to get through the emotional family issues that are inevitable when you own a business together. Family meetings are sometimes painful – they stir up old memories and conflicts. People have to feel that the central purpose of working through such difficulties is the welfare of the family.

What I like to suggest to business-owning families is that they write a family mission statement and that they think of it as independent of whether or not they own a business. That way, the mission statement is really for the family. Then the family can ask itself, "Does owning a business together make sense, given the family's mission?" This process helps people think through the reasons for owning a business together, and they often discover what other successful families have come to realize: that a business offers many benefits to a family, and treating the business like a business – with the highest professional standards – *is truly good for the family*. Owning a business encourages family members to develop a solid work ethic. They learn that working together for common interests serves the welfare of the family, and that running an exemplary institution and doing something good for others – such as employees or the community – bring pride and credit to the family.

Still, if the family's mission is the welfare of the family, the family has to do things other than own a business together. Its family mission statement can focus, for example, on the importance of being a family and continuing as a family. It may talk of promoting the growth and development of individual family members so that they can achieve their fullest potential, or it can concentrate on creating a legacy of values, making the world a better place, or contributing to the well-being of others.

When the family's mission is central, members begin to ask questions like, "What other things should we be doing as a family for the family, in addition to owning a business together?" That leads to philanthropy, to family education, to providing services for family members through a family office, to establishing policies about family members in need, and to reunions and other family fun. As a result, more family members are involved and the emotional strength of the family increases. Here are two examples of family mission statements (the businesses are fictional). The first, "The Suarez Family Mission Statement" (Figure 6.1), is an excellent representation of the kind of document described in this lesson because it keeps the family in

Our mission is to fulfill our potential as individuals and as a family by appreciating each person for who he or she is and for what each can share with others in the family.

In that spirit, we will:
    support each other's interests, individuality, and initiatives.
    encourage each other's growth in their personal, spiritual, and career aspirations.
    be adventurous as we expand our cultural exposure and knowledge by seeking to explore a bigger world.
    participate in our communities, practice responsible citizenship, and lend our hands to those less fortunate.
    preserve our family as a place of security where we can love and enjoy one another's company.

Our fundamental goal is to safeguard these values for future generations.

Figure 6.1   *The Suarez family mission statement*

Our mission is to provide stewardship for Johansson Consolidated Enterprises, recognizing that through it, we can provide opportunities for growth and prosperity for our family's future generations.

We will accomplish this by supporting the management of the company in its efforts to accomplish the company mission and growth objectives and by educating future generations about the history and values of the family.

FAMILY OBJECTIVES

1. The family is committed to the continuance of the company as a privately held family business.
2. We strive for consensus in family meetings, using the family mission and objectives as guidelines. Individuals will commit to resolving conflict with a "win-win" perspective and to avoid grudges or other relationship-destructive behavior.
3. Decisions will be made in the best interest of the company mission when there is a conflict between personal and business priorities.
4. General information on financial condition, sales, profitability, and company policies will be available to all family members with the understanding that it is not general knowledge to be shared with others.
5. The family recognizes the company traditions of thinking long-term when it comes to managing the business and of allowing management to run the day-to-day operations of the company.
6. We acknowledge the role of the Chairman and Board of Directors having final authority in matters of the business and we recognize that the Board of Directors represents our interests.
7. We see it as one of our roles to actively educate the future generations in the family history and values that made Johansson Consolidated Enterprises a success.

Figure 6.2   *Johansson family mission*

center stage. The second, "Johansson Family Mission" (Figure 6.2), is the kind of statement that could grow out of the first. Note how the Johansson statement defines the relationship of the family to the business.

Lesson 47   Synthesis of Values

Long-lasting family businesses have learned that value systems and people shift over time. In the first and second generations, the value system is very tight because everyone has grown up in the same home; family members all tend to agree upon the same values because they've been acculturated to the same views.

As the family grows larger and there are more branches, greater diversity evolves. In-laws bring other values into the family, and cousins are brought up in different families with different values. The family's original value system diffuses, and there may be a risk of contradictory credos. The business, however, needs a foundation of agreed-upon values to assure its sense of direction and continued high performance. Successful families approach this need in two ways. They consciously and continuously work at the value system, discussing it at family meetings, communicating it to the business, communicating it from the business back to the family, and refining it as appropriate. In this way, they help reduce the amount of diffusion and help shape the diffusion that occurs.

They also understand that it's just inevitable that there will be family members who will feel uncomfortable with the family's value system and who will rebel. If they are owners, this is where Lesson 14, "Graceful Pruning," comes into play, encouraging people with extreme or opposite values to redeem their shares without judgment and making it clear that even though they depart the business, they are still members of the family, loved and appreciated.

Another thing that long-lasting business families come to understand about values: In the first and second generations, values tend to be very normative and may be expressed in authoritarian, exclusionary ways – for example, in principles like, "All family members will be raised in and belong to the Presbyterian church," or "All the family's charitable contributions will remain in our community." In later generations, when the family gets to be quite large, the goal is to try to create a sense of family continuity and solidarity of support for the business. Value statements tend to become more inclusive so as to encompass the increasing diversity of family members. The values articulated may become a little more bland and there may be fewer of them, but the focus is on what values can be identified that bring people closer together rather than what values the family will insist people hold and by which they will be judged if they don't.

One of the beauties of Stage III is that values now are not only passed back and forth between the family and the business, they are passed back and forth and among and between the family and the many institutions that it has created – several businesses, perhaps, and a family foundation and possibly a family office. The values of one organization reinforce the values of another, institution to institution. At the Ermenegildo Zegna Group, a world leader in fine textiles and menswear based in Trivero, Italy, the fourth-generation family members have been strongly influenced by values and social concerns of the second-generation leader, Ermenegildo Zegna. He was concerned about nature and environmental protection, and one of his philanthropic projects included reforesting the mountains near Trivero. "He was an ecologist well before the word existed!" says his younger son, Angelo Zegna.[31] Following his example, the fourth-generation Zegnas have demonstrated the family's continuing respect for the environment with a reserve of forest and meadows. Intended to promote environmental education, it is overseen by one of the family members. Another family member, Anna Zegna, says that "the family business is a point of reference of values." As she explains, "For the Zegnas, it all started with a social commitment to the small community and the people of Trivero. We pass these values on to our children from generation to generation, and it is the duty of the family to bring these values to the company."[32]

The family that owns Barcelona-based Corporación Puig has developed a Family Handbook that demonstrates how values flow from family to business and back again – on an international scale. The company is famous for such brands as Nina Ricci and Paco Rabanne and has holdings throughout the world. For employees throughout the group, the Family Handbook sets forth the family's expectations in terms of ethics and professional principles. In one instance, managers turned down a proposal for a purported weight-reducing product because selling products that make false claims would be a violation of the Puig family ethics.[33] In a case like this, the family sees its values put into action and can feel reaffirmed in the values choices it has made. In addition, the values-oriented decision of the managers in one business unit can influence other units and reinforce their adherence to the owning family's values (see Figure 6.3).

Another example might be a family that has identified the dignity of the individual as a core value. It not only insists that individual dignity be honored in the way it does business but it also sets up a foundation that researches and champions individual dignity. The research is made available to the public but it also gets fed back into the company and the family so that it can be used to enhance their efforts to respect human dignity. Again, the

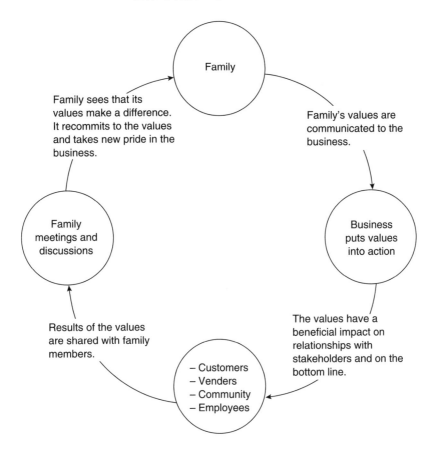

Figure 6.3   *Reinforcing values between family and business*

cross-institutional reinforcement of values in turn strengthens the core value system of the family.

Lesson 48   Social Purpose

Commitment to and enthusiasm for a family business are often tied to a belief that the business really does contribute to society. Making money is important as a resource and it provides a measure of performance, discipline, competitiveness, and competence. However, many successful families believe that the company's reason for being is not just to maximize profits or make money – its deepest purpose is to do something good for people.

A sense of purpose is essential in Stage III, when most of the owners are not working in the business. Believing that the business is not only a marvelous company in its own right but also that it makes a difference to others gives nonactive shareholders a reason to be proud, patient owners, willing to make sacrifices and give of themselves for the sake of the business.

Social purpose can take many forms. Some families find it in creating jobs. They know they are contributing to the stability of the local economy and perhaps providing quality work experiences for people as well.

Philanthropy or charitable activities, as we have seen, also imbue an extended family with a sense of purpose. In many cases, membership in a business-owning family can lead to opportunities to sit on the local or even national boards of charitable organizations, universities, and businesses, providing family members with additional avenues for making contributions to the world around them. In small countries, extended families know that their businesses are influential institutions that are essential to a nation's welfare or that affect its culture. Both Khalid Kanoo of the Y.B.A. Kanoo Group in Bahrain and Jaime Zobel of the Ayala Corporation in the Philippines acknowledge the roles that their family companies have played in developing the infrastructures of nations. In 1969, when he was 27 years old, Kanoo was sent to be assistant branch manager of Y.B.A. Kanoo's office in Abu Dhabi in the United Arab Emirates. Life was tough and amenities such as power and water were lacking. However, Kanoo recalls, "You could see your contribution and you would know that it would be appreciated. I could say to myself, I was the first to import these Hyster fork-life trucks for the port or, those are my tugs operating out there, all helping to build a new country."[34] Zobel observes that as a property developer in an emerging market like the Phillines, Ayala has had to be a "catalyst for the infrastructure needs of the country. ... [giving] people the quality of life they desire: clean running water, say, or efficient transport."[35]

Whatever direction it takes, a sense of purpose, like fun, education, and meaningful roles, helps bond members of an extended family and builds and sustains their support for the business for yet another generation.

Lesson 49   Process is End, Not Means

Throughout these lessons, the examples of long-lasting, successful businesses have encouraged you and your family to develop a variety of policies – employment, mission statement, family code, exit-redemption, and so on. You've been urged to create education programs and estate plans and to hold family retreats, family reunions, and council meetings.

You have been prodded to do many things, but what is essential to remember is that the *process* you as family members go through is as important as – if not more important than – the results. Successful families understand it's not the decisions they come up with, the values they choose, and the accomplishments they make that carry the most weight. It is of greater consequence that they gain skills in working together as family members, and that they seek together, talk together, learn together, struggle together, get to know one another better, grow more tolerant of one another, and learn how to come to agreement as a group. These are the kinds of things that happen as they engage in such processes as developing policies, doing collaborative planning, enjoying a family reunion, or setting philanthropic goals.

Because process is so important, successful families make the assumption that whatever policies or statements they create today can be changed three years or five years or a generation from now. Some families believe that policies should have sunset clauses, perhaps extinguishing them every generation. They tell the next generation, sometimes in a preamble, "These policies are important to us and work for us, but if you just embrace them as they are, you will miss the most important part: going through the process of creating your own."

Konrad Henkel, the wise third-generation leader of the Henkel Group, built on the tradition of family unity established by his grandfather when in 1994 he invited the 60 members of the fourth and fifth generations to start making plans for the role of the family as owners in the future. The third-generation family members stepped back as the younger people conducted a series of meetings and discussions on whether the business should be sold, what the governance should be, and other topics. The process took nearly two years but by the end, they had developed a new 20-year shareholder agreement, one that committed them to continued family ownership of Henkel and provided family shareholders with more influence on company mission and strategy.[36]

Lesson 50   Family Business Advocate

Way back in Lesson 1, we talked about social entrepreneurs – founders who, among other things, are active in the world of ideas and love to share with others what they have learned, especially about management. This lesson brings the extended family full circle back to that notion. Instead of sharing philosophies and experiences about entrepreneurship and management, however, the family shares its enthusiasm for and knowledge about family business with other families and the broader world.

Granted, many old, successful business-owning families are very private and do not go in this direction. Many others, however, believe so thoroughly in the value of family business to society that they become its advocates.

Some welcome other families to visit them, and they share their stories openly with their guests. Others become proponents of legislation that will benefit family business and acknowledge the importance of its role in society. The largest, oldest, most successful family companies in Spain were the ones that brought about changes in the estate-tax laws to support family business continuity in their country.

Some families fund research in family business, or they provide financial support to family business educational centers, such as those at colleges and universities. In other instances, they share themselves, agreeing to speak about their experiences at seminars, conferences, and other events. At my own school, IMD, we have been fortunate to benefit from the financial and personal support of the 200-year-old Lombard Odier Darrier Hentsch family-led private banks and the Wild Group's investment in our family business education endeavors.

Such advocacy brings benefits back to the family. When family members "go public" with the lessons they have learned, it helps strengthen or revitalize their commitment to what they have focused on for so long – the family and the business. By sharing what they know with other families, they renew their own beliefs and they practice a form of public accountability.

A TALE OF TWO FAMILIES (CONT.)

Sadly, this is no longer "a tale of two families." The Bingham family business, as we have seen, disintegrated in Stage II with the failure of the fractious siblings to form not only an effective partnership but also any partnership at all.

The Sulzbergers, however, marched on to Stage III. The Ochs Trust was automatically dissolved on Iphigene's death and four new trusts were created – one for each of the siblings (now in their 60s and 70s) and their descendants. "All their adult lives [the siblings] had complained about being perceived as rich without having the bank accounts to back it up," note Tifft and Jones. Now each owned *New York Times* stock worth more than $80 million.[37]

At a very early age, Arthur Ochs Sulzberger Jr., Punch's son, knew he wanted to succeed his father as publisher of *The New York Times*. He graduated from Tufts in 1974, and after stints at *The Raleigh Times* in North Carolina and the Associated Press in London, he joined *The New York Times* in 1978 as a reporter, continuing the long, steady climb toward his goal.

He was not alone. There were four other cousins in the business, some with similar ambitions. Punch watched out for their training and promotions as well. Nevertheless, as time went by and Arthur Jr., mentored by non-family executives, advanced to assistant publisher and then deputy publisher.

The company's board of directors had long included not just Punch, his sisters, and high-ranking *Times* executives, but also CEOs and former CEOs of other corporations. When in late 1991 Punch announced his plan to step down as publisher and name his son to the post, the outside directors balked – they wanted to know Arthur Jr. better. Within months, however, they were convinced that Arthur Jr. was the right choice and he was officially appointed at age 40, in 1992. Punch had put his son through a solid training program lasting many years, and, say Tifft and Jones, Arthur Jr. "was the most thoroughly prepared publisher *The New York Times* had ever had."[38] Punch retained the titles of chairman and CEO and, ever mindful of the feelings of the cousins, however, he refused his son's request for a seat on the board.[39]

The five cousins in the business began to launch some startling initiatives. One of them, supported by their parents, was a series of family meetings that would include all 13 cousins, their spouses, and grown children. The purpose was to discuss all of the issues facing their generation, including board membership and how members of the fifth generation would be absorbed into the business.[40]

Until then, the siblings had assumed that when they retired, each would choose a child to fill his or her seat on the board. However, before the family meetings ensued, they met with Craig Aronoff, a family business advisor and educator who had been selected as the facilitator for the meeting process. "Are you one family or four families?" Aronoff asked them. With that question, they began to realize that while they thought of themselves as one family, they were behaving like four families.[41]

The sessions got off the ground in May 1994. The younger family members formed committees on such topics as board succession, family employment policy, and philanthropy, and in early 1995, they presented the siblings with a 50-page document offering their proposals for the future. In it, they pledged that their role as guardian of *The New York Times* would take "precedence over most considerations of individual welfare"[42] and they announced their desire to consider themselves one family instead of four branches.

The "one family" concept led to the remarkable decision to combine the siblings' four separate trusts, which held 85 percent of the voting stock, into one trust from which each of the cousins and their children would inherit equally. For the two cousins in the smallest branch of the family, this meant a significant financial sacrifice – they would have inherited considerably more than their cousins under the old arrangement. But as one of them put it, his brother and he "have made it not an issue of wealth; we've made it an issue of the mission of the newspaper and of the company."[43]

The Sulzbergers also agreed that while there should always be some family members on the board of directors, they did not have to represent each family line, nor did there necessarily have to be four. In 1997, Arthur Jr. was comfortably given the board seat that he had been denied five years earlier.[44]

Punch had yet to fully retire and give up his roles as chairman and CEO of the company. After much discussion with key family members and consultants, he arrived at a plan that the family and the board would accept. Ultimately, Arthur Jr. added the title of company chairman to his role as publisher of *The New York Times*. His cousin, Michael Golden, was named vice chairman and a board director, and a trusted non-family executive was appointed CEO. Before the decisions were announced, Punch took the time to phone or visit each of the cousins to explain his choices.[45]

This chapter identifies 24 lessons that are essential in Stage III, the Cousin Collaboration. A quick scan of these lessons suggests that the Ochs-Sulzbergers have formally or informally put most of them in place. Two that particularly stand out are Lesson 31, Infinite Time Horizon, and Lesson 33, Impersonal Ownership. In their 1986 buy-back agreement, a pact that would guarantee family control of *The New York* Times for another century, the third-generation siblings and their offspring came about as close as you can to institutionalizing an Infinite Time Horizon.

That same document also formalized the concept of Impersonal Ownership. If Class B voting shares were offered back to the family or the company but not purchased by either, the owning family member could sell them to an outsider only after they were converted to less-valuable, ordinary Class A shares. When told that limiting their ability to sell Class B shares on the open market could cost the family as much as $1 billion, the members didn't flinch.[46] Family control of the *Times* outweighed considerations of family or personal wealth. The cousins and their children underscored their commitment to Impersonal Ownership when they decided nearly a decade later to consolidate the four family trusts into one and to share wealth and control equally.

The 1986 agreement also exemplifies Lesson 32, Fair, Facilitated Redemption Freedom, by making it possible for family members to redeem their shares and stipulating the conditions under which such shares could be sold.

Let me call attention to just one more of the lessons that the Sulzbergers exemplify so well – Lesson 45, One Family. Coached by Iphigene, the third-generation siblings practiced the principle of "one for all and all for one." The fourth and fifth generations committed themselves to the one-family concept in their 1995 proposals.

One of the most significant themes to emerge from the lessons in this chapter is that if the family business is to continue long into the future, the family, in Stage III, finds ways to bring its members together as owners and as family. It creates a sense of community in which family members, feeling welcomed and loved and a part of something larger than themselves, enthusiastically and willingly make the sacrifices of time, effort, and even money to support and nurture the family heirloom – its business.

7 Taking the Longest View

Perhaps the Ochs-Sulzberger family owes more to Julius Adler than it realizes. Remember Julius? He was Iphigene's cousin, the one who lost out in the race to become the leader of The New York Times Company following the death of Adolph Ochs. Although he had been bequeathed the financial resources to leave the company if he wanted to and certainly had the ability to succeed elsewhere, he swallowed his disappointment and worked loyally for the family business the rest of his life.

Whether or not the family was conscious of it, Julius set a powerful example for the members of the following generations and the kinds of decisions they would make about the business and their relationship to it and to one another. He demonstrated that you can remain committed to the family business, even if it doesn't satisfy your dearest ambition. He was willing to put the good of the family and the good of the business ahead of his own personal welfare. He showed that you can have respect for other family members and work with them, even though they may have been instrumental in your disappointment – as long as they acted with the good of the business in mind and showed respect in return. He understood the need for the selflessness and sacrifice that go into making a family enterprise great and enduring. Even though Julius was never the business's top leader – perhaps *because* he was never the business's top leader – he embodied valuable attitudes and traits that would help keep the family united and focused into the fifth generation.

I do not mean to dwell on Julius, but I do think it is useful to consider the significant, constructive roles many family members play in a family business, even if they are not the family leader or the business leader. All family members, whether or not they are employed in the business or hold a seat on the board or even own stock, can be significant forces for helping the family understand and put in place the lessons that lead to long-term success.

We have looked at the Bingham and Ochs-Sulzberger families and how they did or did not absorb many of the 50 Lessons as their businesses evolved. Let us now explore these two families and some of the many others you have met in these pages from the perspective of the over-arching principles we examined in Chapter 2 – The Five Insights and The Four P's.

First, the Five Insights:

Insight #1: We Respect the Challenge

Adolph Ochs knew from the day he owned his very first enterprise that he was in business for his family. As time went on, he knew that he wanted his business to pass on not just to his daughter but, as specified in his will, to his grandchildren. Initially, he probably had limited understanding of how hard passing on a business could be, but his realization grew as he was faced with a succession decision that made rivals of his son-in-law and his nephew.

As the business and family both became larger and more complex, each generation grew more sophisticated in its respect for the challenge. Children were deliberately educated on the responsibilities of ownership, values were inculcated that would help hold the family together so that it could support and guide the business, and various documents were drawn up to help assure family control well into the future. The 1986 buy-back agreement, in particular, signaled that the signers understood that family members in the future might not be at peace with one another but that, despite disagreements, the document would help assure the continuity of family control for generations to come.

Judge Bingham did not likely think of himself as the head of a "family" business. He passed leadership and controlling ownership of the business on to the only son capable of running it, Barry Bingham Sr. As we have seen, Barry Sr. and his wife, Mary, intended to do much the same – pass the business on to a son who would lead and have controlling ownership. Perhaps that seemed simple enough, given the relative ease of transition from Judge Bingham to Barry Sr. However, they were stunned when the heir apparent died an untimely death. Nor did they consider, until much too late, the roles that their minority-shareholder daughters would or could play – they raised sons to run the business, not daughters. The challenge of passing on a family business, as the Binghams learned, is very hard indeed, and sometimes excruciatingly cruel.

Families that respect the challenge and develop sophistication about it increase their chances of perpetuating the businesses they own as family businesses. Consider again the Henkel Group. One of the reasons Konrad Henkel relinquished leadership in 1980 at the age of 65, despite being in good health, was that he wanted to devote himself to developing a governance structure that would assure the growth and future of the family business. He and his contemporaries in the family created such a structure. In addition, Konrad provided guidance and inspiration to the two generations that followed as they struggled to define their relationship to the business they owned. He also fostered family unity, and encouraged commitment to the business among the younger family members through such activities as group visits to Henkel facilities around the world.[1]

In other words, the Henkel family has been deliberate in its respect for the challenge of perpetuating a business through many generations of family ownership. Many of the long-lasting family businesses in this book demonstrate a similar deliberateness – Codorníu, for example, as well as Murugappa Group, and S.C. Johnson & Son.

Insight #2: Family Business Issues are Common and Predictable, and Perspectives on the Same Issues will be Different

Neither the Ochs-Sulzberger family or the Binghams understood the commonality and predictability of family business issues at the outset, and most Bingham family members never did gain such understanding. By the 1980s, Barry Jr. had certainly begun to understand, and he knew families in trouble could benefit from the outside help that was steadily becoming available to family firms. However, he was rebuffed when he tried to persuade others in the family that hiring a family business advisor or bringing outsiders to the board would be useful. The Binghams certainly offered differing perspectives on any given issue, but the distrust among family members, dating back to the third-generation siblings' childhood, was so great that respect for other points of view and empathy for one another were virtually nonexistent.

Respect for differing perspectives in the Ochs-Sulzberger family began with Adolph Ochs. At times, he urged his daughter, Iphigene, to temper her dogmatism. "One of his greatest gifts," observe Tifft and Jones, "was the ability to see an issue from all sides, to disassociate himself from the passion surrounding a subject and, instead, examine it as though it were a specimen under a microscope."[2]

The Sulzbergers, like Barry Bingham Jr., came to understand that family businesses shared issues in common and were predictable. It was a realization that enabled the family to turn to professional family business advisors for help in implementing a successful transition from the Sibling Partnership to the Cousin Collaboration.

So, too, do other families appreciate the commonality of family businesses and take steps to build on their strengths and avoid their typical pitfalls. Recognizing that many family businesses stumble because of harmful rivalries, the Kanoo family attempts to give its young people a chance to work together as friends and to nurture a sense of shared success. "If the young generation think along the lines that 'Fawzi's achievement is Saud's achievement' or 'Yusuf's achievement is Ali's achievement' then we shall continue to complement each other and not compete jealously," explains Khalid Kanoo.[3]

Sonepar, the French electrical equipment distributor, understands and capitalizes on the second part of Insight #2 – that family members will have differing perspectives. Because Sonepar started out as a business forged by two families, each with different strengths, family members learned generations ago how to make partnerships work. Sonepar now uses that knowledge to make sure its relationships with the companies it acquires are successful ones. "Among other things, we learned that durability could only be achieved by rising above diverging attitudes," said Henri Coisne, Sonepar's former chairman. A respect for individuality, he added, "has enabled us to have greater tolerance for the idiosyncrasies of the companies we have bought." As a result, he said, "consideration for our partners comes naturally."[4]

Insight #3: Communication is Indispensable

Communication in neither the Ochs-Sulzberger family nor the Bingham family was perfect. Fathers and sons in the Sulzberger family had a particularly hard time relating to one another. Some of the family rules – avoiding conflict, for example – were obstacles to honesty and openness.

However, Punch took the need for communication very seriously. He assiduously kept his sisters informed about the business and sought their counsel. After his father's death, his mother, Iphigene, became his confidante and advisor, and he met with her every weekend in private. He talked with family members and board members individually when he felt his thinking needed to be explained.

In the 1990s, the cousins began to institutionalize forums for communication. The five cousins in the business began meeting on their own and eventually launched the series of family meetings that would open up communication with all the cousins, their spouses, and their children.

In the Bingham family, communication was nothing short of disaster. The family had, but misused, the two pillars of family business communication – family meetings and the board of directors. The board lacked the outside directors so essential to it. And while the family met frequently during the waning of its business ownership, the meetings were often venues for promoting individual self-interest and finding something else to fight about.

Again, distrust was an obstacle, and family members were not schooled in the skills and requirements of communication: empathy, the art of listening, compromise, and so on.

Communication patterns in the Gucci family also left much to be desired. Sons were expected to "listen" to their fathers and to obey, not question, no matter how old a son might be. Of Aldo's three sons, Paolo in particular could not tolerate this aspect of his relationship with his father. He further resented the senior generation's lack of communication about the financial aspects of the business. As a result, he became the dissident family member and, eventually, the target of Maurizio and the outside investors seeking to wrest control from Aldo's branch of the family. They were looking for the weakest link, and Paolo, disaffected from the family and its business, was it.[5]

Insight #4: Planning is Essential to Continuity

The initial discussion of this insight points out that long-lasting, successful family businesses do planning on four levels, putting together a Business Strategy Plan, a Leadership and Ownership Succession Plan, a Personal Financial Plan for family members, and a Family Continuity Plan. The Ochs-Sulzberger clan gets high marks on most counts, with some generations doing better than others at one plan or another. Adolph Ochs, for example, was a master strategist, and although he came up with an ownership plan, he failed to join it with a map for leadership. Throughout the generations, business strategy would be a strong point. It was rooted in the core notion that excellent journalism would lead to financial success, a concept flexible enough to permit pursuing a range of tactics at given times, from providing more columns of news in a period when rivals were cutting back to embarking on a series of acquisitions in another era.

Except for Adolph Ochs's early life, financial security was generally not an issue until the third generation, when Iphigene's longevity and her father's will resulted in the siblings' occasional dependence on Iphigene for financial help. Once the siblings came into their own inheritances, the matter, for the time, was resolved.

The Sulzberger cousins and their children appear to have beautifully addressed the Family Continuity Plan with the proposals they presented to the siblings in 1995. They dealt not only with how they wanted to share ownership, but they also looked at issues ranging from governance and philanthropy to employment in the business. It was a watershed document.

The Binghams had a goal – to create a great Southern liberal newspaper – and they achieved it. They, too, based their strategy on presenting the highest quality journalism but, in contrast to the Sulzbergers, they did not use it as a springboard for launching other strategies. When the company was sold, its holdings were largely the same as they were when Judge Bingham ran the company in the 1920s: two newspapers, a broadcast station, and a printing company. Outsiders on the board might have helped the Binghams envision a bolder, longer-range strategy but outsiders were not welcome to board seats.

Mary and Barry Bingham Sr. were financially secure – what kind of plan they had created for themselves, we do not know. Despite their security, however, Barry Sr. never gave up his controlling ownership and no plan for transferring it was in evidence.

The Binghams never got near to putting together a Family Continuity Plan. They couldn't even agree on a statement articulating goals for their business.[6]

Again, the Y.B.A. Kanoo Group, where planning on many levels gets frequent attention, offers a helpful example. While strategic planning and planning for family continuity at Kanoo Group are similar to what business-owning families in Europe and North America would find familiar, other aspects of planning are not, because they are shaped by Arab and Muslim culture. Financial security is handled quite differently. As noted earlier, married male family members who work in the business receive similar salaries and housing. By custom, wives also receive similar salaries and allowances to cover household and personal needs, but the amount varies somewhat according to circumstance. If a wife has two children, for example, she will receive more than a wife who has not yet started a family. A percentage is set aside from the business for a family fund that covers education, housing, travel, and holidays.[7] Two brothers owned the company 50–50 in the third generation. As a show of love for one another, the seven sons who joined the business in the fourth generation decided to share their combined inheritance equally, though this meant less for sons in the smaller branch than they would have received otherwise.[8] In matters of inheritance, the Kanoos, as Muslims, abide by Shari`a Law, under which what one receives is determined by a well-defined formula.[9] The inheritors, however, can decide how they want to share their inheritance, as did the fourth-generation sons. Under this system, everyone knows what to expect.

Khalid Kanoo relates that he received two-thirds of his father's inheritance and his sister received one-third. "To make the running of the company's affairs easier, my sister gave me a power-of-attorney to act on her behalf."[10] The disparity of their legacies reflects the male's obligation to be the breadwinner and to look after not just his immediate family but also extended family members when necessary.

Insight #5: Commitment is Required of Us

The Binghams – especially Mary, Barry Sr., and Barry Jr. – loved *The Courier-Journal* and were proud of what it represented in the newspaper world. But love and pride in a family business are not the same as commitment to its future in the family. In the end, the family as a whole could not answer the key question: "How does owning a business make sense to our family?"

The commitment of the Ochs-Sulzbergers was present from the beginning and spread contagiously to the new family members in each generation. *The New York Times*, the heart of the business, was and still is seen as a public trust, and family members today understand that it is their privilege and their duty to preserve it so that the next generation, in turn, can also have the privilege of serving as its guardian.

And now, the Four P's:

Policies Before the Need

Neither the Binghams nor the Ochs-Sulzbergers seem to score well in this regard. With their 1995 proposals, the fourth and fifth generations of Sulzbergers appear to be finally setting down guidelines for the family as it relates to the business. Considering how many family members have been hired over the years primarily because they were family members or in-laws, it would have been helpful long ago to have at least had an employment policy governing family participation in the business. As it was, some family members had inflated expectations about what their future role would be.

The only policy we have evidence of in the Bingham enterprises was an ethics code that was instituted by Barry Jr. and which won national praise. It was not a family policy per se, but it affected the family, making it clear that family members would be reported on like anyone else, and that everyone working for the newspapers, including family members, was subject to conflict-of-interest rules that prevented employee participation in many civic groups. The latter angered Sallie, who worked for a time as *The Courier-Journal's* book editor and had to resign from a lobbying committee.[11] Barry Sr. disagreed with the idea of having a written conflict-of-interest policy at all.[12] Perhaps family members would have felt more warmly toward an ethics policy had they had the opportunity to participate in its creation.

Contrast the Binghams with Hermès, where there are policies stipulating that family members can join the company only if they're professionally competent, and that payment of dividends is guided by the needs of the company, not the needs of shareholders.[13] Or with Puig family, which not only created the Family Handbook mentioned earlier, but also developed a "Family Protocol" governing how the family will relate to the business. It sets forth conditions for family members who want to work in the business, and includes many rules, such as one prohibiting in-laws from serving on the company's executive board and another barring the use of shares as collateral.[14]

Sense of Purpose

A sense of purpose goes hand-in-hand with commitment because it gives the family a reason for that commitment. As we have discussed, the Ochs-Sulzbergers have believed for more than a century that The New York Times represents a purpose larger than any single member of the family. There is almost a religious fervor about their belief in the Times and their duty, as a family, to preserve and protect it.

A sense of purpose would be neither so widespread nor so long-lasting in the Bingham family. Perhaps it was felt most strongly by Mary and Barry Sr. when he was running the business and *The Courier-Journal* was the center of their attention. Barry Jr. certainly experienced it as well. But it was not inculcated in the daughters, who, at least in their childhood and early adulthood, were not expected to participate in the business.

Process

It is clear that the members of many of the enduring business families introduced in this book have been willing to do the hard work that process involves. You may recall that process, by my definition, means all the thinking and meeting and discussing that family members do together to resolve issues. Successful process requires certain skills, including communicating, problem solving, and the ability to collaborate and reach consensus. It also requires that family members respect one another and that each be able to put the welfare of the business and the family ahead of one's own personal interests.

Members of the Gucci family and the Steinberg family not only lacked the skills to engage in process successfully, but they seemed to lack the respect and concern for one another's welfare that would be necessary to make process work. Remember, for example, that Aldo felt that his brother Rodolfo didn't make a contribution worth his 50 percent ownership – an attitude that was transferred, with deleterious effects, to Aldo's sons. Remember, also, that the sons in the Gucci family were expected to take orders but not necessarily to have their opinions and ideas heard. The Steinberg daughters seemed unable to listen to one another either, nor to understand the role their father had played in creating the unhappy situation in which they found themselves – by discouraging them from getting higher educations and by setting up trusts that would make them unwillingly dependent on one another.

The Ochs-Sulzbergers showed time and time again that they were not only willing to work through process, they were also *able*. They took care to develop the skills that were necessary, sometimes hiring consultants to help them work through difficult issues. The Binghams were certainly willing to engage in process but they lacked the skills and attitudes to do it effectively.

Parenting

Such a touchy subject! In both the Bingham and Ochs-Sulzberger families, no doubt about it, the second-generation parents loved their children. But both sets of parents were caught up in a whirl of work and the social life it engendered, and their privileged children suffered a form of neglect. Who can explain why one set of siblings became fractious while the other grew united? Let me suggest some possible factors. The Ochs-Sulzbergers had a very strong sense of family. There were often extended family members living with the Ochses, and even after Iphigene grew up, she and her family were expected to spend time with Adolph and his wife on the weekends.15 The sense of family also ran deep in the business. Even though Adolph deprived Iphigene of the opportunity of working in the business, he gave her great power in it by making her one of the three trustees of the Ochs trust. And clearly, because the trust was to pass on to Iphigene's four children, Adolph had a vision for the company that encompassed multiple children in future generations.

With the Binghams, the idea of family was not nearly so strong. Barry Sr.'s early family life had been shattered with the death of his mother when he was a child, and he was not very close to his own brother and sister. For her part, Mary had left her family behind in Richmond, and there was not a passel of cousins nearby for the Bingham children to grow up with or enjoy. If the business stayed in the family, control and leadership were expected to go to one of the sons. There would be none of the messiness of involving sisters and cousins and in-laws. Family was secondary.

Perhaps because of their patrilineal outlook, Barry and Mary thought it unnecessary to groom their children for ownership, even though Judge Bingham had left each of them a small stake in the company. In any case, Mary and Barry Sr. did nothing that we know of to educate the children for ownership. Nor did these parents recognize the disunity among the children while they were still young. If they had, perhaps they could have taken steps to counteract the animosity.

These are speculations, of course, and perhaps you will see other factors at work in these families and draw other conclusions.

As I reflect on the 50 Lessons that I have learned from enduring family businesses, it seems to me that parenting infuses every one of them. Many of the lessons involve the parents' direct guidance of the offspring. For example, under Lesson 4, Principle of Merit, children learn what expectations they must meet to enter and rise in the business. In Lesson 10, Understated Wealth, and Lesson 11, Wealth is Neutral, parents pass on healthy attitudes toward wealth. In Lesson 39, Family Education, they see to it that their children have the opportunity to learn some valuable lessons that prepare them for life.

But all the lessons, even where the parent–offspring relationship is not so clear or direct, are parenting lessons in that the senior generation is setting an example for the next generation. When Owner/Managers hire talented executives from outside the family and reward them well (Lessons 6 and 7), they demonstrate to their children the value of doing so. When the brothers and sisters in a Sibling Partnership take the time to learn communication skills and make communication education available to other family members (Lesson 21), they are sending a message to their children that good communication is essential to the family and its business. When the shareholding cousins in Stage III take an interest in the business and do what they can to support it even though they don't work in it, they're showing the next generation that it's important to be an enlightened, responsible owner. Every lesson here gives someone the opportunity to be a role model for a younger family member.

Let us return for a moment to the Smorgon family, which decided to divest itself of its conglomerate, Smorgon Consolidated Industries (SCI), in 1995. It followed through on this plan. Nevertheless, it is still a family in business together. SCI's holdings – meat, plastic containers, paper mills, and more – sold quickly until only the steel business was left. The family decided to expand it and make it ready to take public when the timing was right.[16] That moment came in 1999 when 33 percent of Smorgon Steel was sold to new investors while the family retained 67 percent. Graham Smorgon, in the family's third generation, became chairman of the board, and other family members, including a fourth-generation member, Peter Edwards, also sat on the board.[17]

Despite how smoothly the decision to sell was made and how quickly the family enterprises found new owners, the events were hard on Victor Smorgon, the Stage II leader. The business had been a center of his life since he was a young teenager. Breaking it up left him despondent.

As his biographer, Rod Myer, observes, it was the "ebbing of Victor's life's purpose. Without the family working together his life had little meaning." His dream, says Myer, "had been to create a dynasty ... that would last 200 years or more."[18]

Victor overcame his depression, and, despite his advancing years, he found a new way to work with his family. He set up a new business, Victor Smorgon Group, to invest the proceeds of the SCI breakup in and partner with business ventures initiated by his grandchildren. His grandson, Peter Edwards (the one who sits on the Smorgon Steel board), became managing director and Victor became executive chairman. His four daughters were named directors.[19] Victor Smorgon Group has since expanded its mission to include partnerships outside the family.[20] Nevertheless, it first and foremost enables Victor to follow his passion: encouraging the members of his family to work together.

It's my hope that, as you've read these chapters, you've given thought many times over to your own family business, reflecting about what stage it is in, what issues and problems you share in common with other family firms in the same stage, and what lessons you already have in place or need to implement. You have also seen how interlinked the lessons are with one another and with the over-arching principles. If you take a look at Appendix B, "Integrating the Lessons," you will see one way of grouping the 50 Lessons under the umbrellas of the Five Insights and the Four P's. Even if you think these elements should be plotted differently, what's important is that every lesson and every principle is related to other lessons and principles. Sometimes, one cannot stand without the other. It's almost impossible, for example, to talk about commitment without having a sense of purpose to be committed to. Or to think about wealth as neutral without thinking about the parenting that goes into making that concept a reality.

Whatever stage your business is in, you now have some important tools to employ in increasing your chances of success in reaching the next stage. As you put those tools to use, take the longest view you can. Examine what you are thinking of doing today in light of how it will affect your family's business and your children's children and consider the possible secondary consequences that might result.

The lessons offered here are not my lessons. They reflect what real families have learned in order to make their businesses enduring and successful. The families in these pages are the teachers here, for you and for me. Especially so are the families I have learned from who are not mentioned directly in this book. I hope they know who they are and how much I have gleaned from them and how much they instruct others.

Let me express special appreciation again to Susan E. Tifft and Alex S. Jones for their great and comprehensive case histories of the

Ochs-Sulzberger and Bingham families. Stories have so much to teach us, and these accounts of these two families are rich with insight.

Families sharing experiences with other business families and with students like me offer hope to all. What they share makes all the 50 Lessons possible and provides the living example that families in business can be long-lasting and successful both as business owners and as families. They hold out the promise that "our children's children" will reap the benefits of and in their turn become the stewards of the legacies that their thoughtful and caring forebears have left them.

Appendix A: The Lessons at a Glance

Use this section when you need a quick review of the 50 Lessons. B = Essential from a Business Perspective, and F = Essential from a Family Perspective.

STAGE I: OWNER-MANAGED STAGE

1. [B] Social Entrepreneurs. Leaders are able to take their businesses through several waves of strategic renewal. They have an "incompletable mission," believe they are the creators and developers of a philosophy of management, are active in the world of ideas, and see themselves as stewards of their businesses.
2. [B] Irrevocable Retirement. A fixed retirement age is evenhandedly applied to everyone in the company, including the CEO.
3. [B] Voluntary Accountability. Leaders know they perform better when they are held accountable. They put mechanisms in place, such as an independent board of directors, to foster accountability.
4. [B] Principle of Merit. Policies are adopted that focus on competence and earned privilege and discourage paternalism in the business. The family makes clear that a principle of merit is part of its value system so that family members know what is expected of them if they wish to join and rise in the business.
5. [B] Attract Most Competent Family Members. The business is run in a professional manner to make it attractive to the most able members of the next generation. The family recognizes that its most competent members have opportunities elsewhere and don't want the burden of carrying incompetent family members.
6. [B] Many Non-Family Executives. Owners create opportunities and space for talented outsiders. They make their business more competitive by structuring it to accommodate both family and non-family executives.
7. [B] Opportunities for Wealth. Prized non-family executives are given opportunities to create personal wealth over and above a good income. Owners use bonuses, phantom stock, and other means to express appreciation to excellent non-family executives for all they have done and are doing for the business-owning family.

8. [F] Family First Environment. Owners recognize that the family is more important than the business. They make time for family interests and fun apart from the business – without compromising the business.

9. [F] Family Business Student. Family members educate themselves about family business by reading, attending seminars, and visiting other family businesses.

10. [F] Understated Wealth. Members of the wealth-creating generation live beneath their means, setting an example of saving and planning for one's own financial security.

11. [F] Wealth is Neutral. Wealth is neither shown off nor hidden. The family recognizes that wealth doesn't make people better people nor is wealth seen as a source of evil. Children understand the family has money and learn that wealth was the result of effort.

STAGE II: THE SIBLING PARTNERSHIP

12. [B] Graceful Pruning. The family makes it easy for members to sell their shares and does not stigmatize those who no longer want to be owners. It feels ownership is best concentrated among people of like goals and values who can move the company forward.

13. [B] Leverage Strengths of Being Private. Family business strengths such as trust, long-term orientation, and an ability to make quick decisions are recognized and exploited as competitive advantages.

14. [B] Invest in Social Capital. The business family finds ways to invest in and support its community and knows it will be strengthened by the resulting good will.

15. [B] Business Bias. Business and family are seen as interdependent and mutually supportive. It is assumed that what is good for the business also serves the best interest of the family.

16. [B] Selective Family Employment. Employment policies are developed carefully to encourage only the most competent family members to join the business. Policies are thoroughly communicated to the family.

17. [F] Open Disclosure/Transparency. The sibling partners build and maintain trust by practicing open disclosure in three areas: (1) Compensation, perks, and benefits; (2) Outside investment opportunities; and (3) Personal estate plans.

18. [F] Aggressive Gifting. To minimize the estate taxes that come with a business that is growing in value, siblings gift shares as much as they can, as soon as they can, to children and grandchildren.

19. [F] Next Generation Early Education. Recognizing that their children may become employees and/or owners of the business one day, parents expose them early to the business and educate them about it – without pressuring them

to join. Parents also educate the children in family process skills such as listening and communicating.

20. [F] Family Code. Family members develop an agreement that states how they will treat one another and how they will conduct themselves with the world outside the family.

21. [F] Communication Skills. Family members invest time and effort into learning communication skills, such as listening, making presentations, confrontational skills, and meeting management and facilitation skills. The wisest families learn as a group.

22. [F] Financial "Nest Eggs." The family sees to it that its members, by young middle age, have their own substantial financial nest eggs. Doing so frees them from being dependent on the senior generation and the business, gives them the opportunity to make free choices about their lives, and provides them dignity.

23. [F] Shared Investments. Siblings recognize that sharing investment opportunities with one another builds trust and helps hold the sibling team together.

24. [F] Educate In-Laws. The business-owning family sensitively educates in-laws in such matters as family culture, the nature of the business, and family agreements (family policies, shareholders agreements, etc.). Doing so helps build in-law support for the family and its enterprise.

25. [F] Legacy of Values. The family links its values to its enterprise, demonstrating to the next generation that traits like honesty, integrity, and respect can enhance the business. The effectiveness of such values in the business reinforces the family's commitment to the values it holds.

26. [F] Successor to "Mom." The business family plans for the continuity of the role of family leadership, whether that role is played by "Mom" or someone else. The family leader is seen as essential to holding the family together emotionally, performing such functions as keeping channels of communication open, educating in-laws, serving as a mediator, and the like.

STAGE III: THE COUSIN COLLABORATION

27. [B] Tradition of Change; Flexible Culture. The cousins reshape the company culture into one that is flexible and that encourages change. They are attuned to the need for ongoing strategic transformation and know that innovation is essential to long-term success.

28. [B] Spirit of Enterprise. The family believes it is "in the business of business." It does not lock itself into the business of origin but maintains an entrepreneurial spirit that enables the business to grow and prosper, encourages family members to start other ventures (including philanthropic ones), and imbues the family with a sense of purpose.

29. [B] Creative Capital. Stage III families find new ways to meet the capital demands of their expanding businesses and growing families. They adapt their

businesses (such as shifting to strategies that are less capital-intensive) or modify their attitudes in ways that allow them to choose paths they have not used before to gain access to capital (such as going public).

30. [B] Flexible Dividend Policies. Dividends are thought of as variable, tying them to profits and reflecting the business's real ability to pay. Family shareholders are educated about how dividends work and how paying out distributions affects the growth of the company.

31. [B] Infinite Time Horizon. Family owners take the attitude that "this business will last forever." They position the business for the long, long-term instead of intermediate-term or short-term gain.

32. [B] Fair, Facilitated Redemption Freedom. The family formalizes a process that allows family owners to redeem some or all of their shares under certain conditions at a fair price. The rules apply to all.

33. [B] Impersonal Ownership. Family shareholders detach themselves from thinking of their stock as a personal, physical asset and focus instead on the welfare of the total family-and-business system. Management is freed to concentrate on doing what's right for the distant future.

34. [F] Family Meetings. Meetings are held regularly to focus on the interests of the family. Such meetings build family cohesion, enhance its sense of identity as a family, and instill a sense of family purpose.

35. [F] Education for Responsible Ownership. Through systematic programs, present and future shareholders are educated about what it means to be an effective owner – from learning how to read financial statements to protocol in dealing with management. Spouses are often included in these programs.

36. [F] Active, Involved Ownership. Family shareholders see it as a duty to contribute to the value of the business by being informed about it and supportive of its strategy. They serve as cultural ambassadors to the business on behalf of the family and strive to be wise and educated governors.

37. [F] Nose In, Fingers Out. Family shareholders don't overstep their boundaries as owners. They're informed and they're involved, but they don't meddle. They go through proper channels.

38. [F] Respect Managers and Managing. Family members understand that managing a business is a very complex and demanding challenge. They have a profound respect for the array of skills that excellent managers bring to the task.

39. [F] Family Education. Family members are conscientiously educated in three major areas: (1) interpersonal skills; (2) personal growth and development; and (3) family culture and history. Education programs are deliberately attentive to family members as individuals and to the family as a group.

40. [F] Family Member Development Program. Career counseling, vocational aptitude testing, and coaching are offered to young people considering careers in the family business. Such resources are often extended to young people interested in other careers, and to older family members as well.

41. [F] Family Leadership Succession. The cousins see the family leadership role as even more important than before and pay as much attention to family

leadership succession as they do to business leadership succession. The family leader – which can be an individual or a group, such as a council of elders – looks after all those things the family would do as a family whether or not its members owned a business together.

42. [F] Provide for Family Members "In Need." The family knows that individual members will have personal problems and special needs, and develops a policy about how such events or circumstances are to be handled. The policy is communicated to all family members.
43. [F] Roles for All in Family Association. All family members are seen as valuable, whether or not they are in the business. Meaningful roles are created on the family side for non-business participants, and family leaders are given the same respect and appreciation as business leaders.
44. [F] Family Philanthropy. The family engages in philanthropy as a way to involve family members not working in the business and to demonstrate appreciation for the privilege and abundance it has enjoyed.
45. [F] One Family. Wisely, the cousins realize they do not have to perpetuate their parents' sibling rivalry. They bury the hatchet and learn to move forward as one family – for the benefit of both business and family.
46. [B] Family's Mission Statement is Central. Family members write a mission statement for the family apart from the business. The process builds cohesion in the family, helps members renew their commitment to the family and the business, and helps the family see other things it can be doing as a family, in addition to owning a business together.
47. [F] Synthesis of Values. Values statements are re-articulated so that they are more inclusionary and can encompass a larger, more diverse family. Values are now passed among many institutions: family, family foundation, family office, and many businesses.
48. [F] Social Purpose. The larger, more diverse family coalesces around the belief that the business serves a greater good. This belief sustains the family's commitment to the business.
49. [F] Process is End, Not Means. The process a family goes through with its continuity planning is more important than the decisions it makes. Whether family members are developing policies, holding a family meeting, or planning a reunion, they gain skills in working together, get to know one another better, and learn how to come to agreement as a group.
50. [F] Family Business Advocate. The family shares its enthusiasm for and knowledge about family business with other families and the broader world.

Appendix B: Integrating the Lessons

The Five Insights and The Four P's transcend the three stages of business and each encompasses many of the lessons. The following table illustrates how the lessons might be grouped under and relate to each of the Insights and P's. It also shows where the lessons fall in each stage of a family business.

Table A.B1   *The Five Insights*

1. We respect the challenge

Family business student	Stage I
Next generation early education	Stage II
Educate in-laws	
Tradition of change	Stage III
Impersonal ownership	
Family meetings	
Education for responsible ownership	
Active, involved ownership	
Nose in, fingers out	
Respect managers and managing	
Family education	
Family member development program	
Family leadership succession	
Family business advocate	

2. Family business issues are common and predictable, and perspectives on the same issues will be different

Family business student	Stage I
Graceful pruning	Stage II
Next generation early education	
Educate in-laws	
Flexible dividend policies	Stage III
Fair, facilitated redemption freedom	
Family meetings	
Education for responsible ownership	
Family business advocate	

(*cont'd*)

Table A.B1 *(cont'd)*

---

3. Communication is indispensable
Voluntary accountability   Stage I
Wealth is neutral

Open disclosure   Stage II
Communication skills
Shared investments
Educate in-laws
Legacy of values

Family meetings   Stage III
Family's mission statement is central
Synthesis of values
Process is end, not means

4. Planning is essential to continuity
Irrevocable retirement   Stage I
Voluntary accountability
Attract most competent family members
Many non-family executives
Opportunities for wealth

Leverage strengths of being private   Stage II
Aggressive gifting
Financial "nest eggs"
Shared investments
Successor to "mom"

Tradition of change; flexible culture   Stage III
Creative capital
Infinite time horizon
Impersonal ownership
Family meetings
Family education
Education for responsible ownership
Family member development program
Family leadership succession
Family's mission statement is central
Process is end, not means

5. Commitment is required of us
Social entrepreneurs   Stage I
Voluntary accountability
Family first environment
Family business student

Open disclosure   Stage II
Invest in social capital
Business bias
Family code

                                                        (cont'd)

Table A.B1 *(cont'd)*

Communication skills	
Legacy of values	Stage III
Spirit of enterprise	
Infinite time horizon	
Impersonal ownership	
Education for ownership	
Active, involved ownership	
Family education	
Family leadership succession	
Roles for all in family association	
Family philanthropy	
One family	
Family's mission statement is central	
Synthesis of values	
Social purpose	

Table A.B2   *The Four P's*

1. Policies before the need	
Irrevocable retirement	Stage I
Voluntary accountability	
Principle of merit	
Selective family employment	Stage II
Family code	
Flexible dividend policies	Stage III
Fair, facilitated redemption freedom	
Provide for family members "in need"	
Family philanthropy	
One family	
Family's mission statement is central	
Process is end, not means	
2. Sense of purpose	
Social entrepreneurs	Stage I
Invest in social capital	Stage II
Legacy of values	
Spirit of enterprise	Stage III
Education for responsible ownership	
Active, involved ownership	
Family philanthropy	
Family's mission statement is central	
Synthesis of values	

(cont'd)

Table A.B2 *(cont'd)*

Social purpose	
Family business advocate	
3. Process	
Voluntary accountability	Stage I
Principle of merit	
Selective family employment	Stage II
Open disclosure/transparency	
Family code	
Communication skills	
Flexible dividend policies	Stage III
Fair, facilitated redemption freedom	
Family meetings	
Roles for all in family association	
Family philanthropy	
One family	
Family's mission statement is central	
Synthesis of values	
Process is end, not means	
4. Parenting	
Family first environment	Stage I
Understated wealth	
Wealth is neutral	
Principal of merit	
Next generation early education	Stage II
Communication skills	
Legacy of values	
Successor to "mom"	
Family meetings	Stage III
Family education	
Education for responsible ownership	
Family education	
Family member development program	
Provide for family "in need"	
Family philanthropy	
One family	
Family's mission statement is central	
Synthesis of values	

Appendix C: A Family Business Checklist

The following list represents the attributes and best practices of the most successful, long-lasting business-owning families. Your goal should be to be able to say yes to these questions. Use the list as a guideline to identify strengths and areas that need attention.

	Yes	No	
1.	___	___	Are the business's leaders committed to long-term continuity for societal and philosophic reasons?
2.	___	___	Is there a mandatory retirement age for all executives, especially owners?
3.	___	___	Does the business have an independent, outside board of directors?
4.	___	___	Does the family get together regularly for fun, not just for business reasons?
5.	___	___	Are family owners actively learning about the field of family business?
6.	___	___	Do family members live modestly, beneath their financial means?
7.	___	___	Is the owning family comfortable with its position of wealth – not letting wealth define the family nor fearing the consequences of wealth on the family?
8.	___	___	Are promotions and compensation of family members clearly based on merit?
9.	___	___	Is the business attracting the most business-competent children in the next generation?
10.	___	___	Does the business rely upon an important cadre of non-family executives?
11.	___	___	Are the non-family executives provided with opportunities to gain personal wealth – beyond compensation?
12.	___	___	Does the family openly share information about family member compensation and benefits? Do family members share information with one another about estate plans and gifts?
13.	___	___	Are owners aggressively gifting or distributing shares to the youngest generations?

	Yes	No	
14.	___	___	Are there easy, graceful ways for family members to redeem their ownership if they wish to do so, thereby facilitating pruning of the ownership tree?
15.	___	___	Is the business strategy enhanced with special competitive advantages from being a private, family-owned company – such as long-term orientation, trusted relationships, etc.?
16.	___	___	Does the family generously "give back" to the community to build social goodwill?
17.	___	___	Does the family accept that the business must be run as an excellent business?
18.	___	___	Is the family selective about which family members are qualified to work in the business?
19.	___	___	Is the family providing business education and exposure to the youngest members of the family?
20.	___	___	Does the family have a "Code of Conduct" to strengthen interpersonal relations and expectations?
21.	___	___	Does the family study and practice communication skills?
22.	___	___	Do family members have independent security beyond their ownership shares in the family business?
23.	___	___	Do family members share information about investment opportunities outside the business?
24.	___	___	Does the family have a process to welcome and acculturate new in-laws to the family?
25.	___	___	Does the family have a statement of family values that it hopes to perpetuate?
26.	___	___	Does the family have an identified family leader?
27.	___	___	Is there a process for the selection of family (not business) leadership?
28.	___	___	Does the business's culture encourage quick responsiveness and change?
29.	___	___	Is the family committed to being in the best businesses for the future – even if that means leaving its business of origin?
30.	___	___	Is the business able to use "other people's money" to fund growth and liquidity?
31.	___	___	Does the company have a formal dividend policy that pays out according to profitability?
32.	___	___	Do the family owners have a commitment to each other for the long, long term?
33.	___	___	Do family members have opportunities to serve as ambassadors on behalf of the business?
34.	___	___	Do the family owners feel they hold their stock for the purpose of passing it on to future generations?
35.	___	___	Does the owning family have regular family meetings?

	Yes	No	
36.	___	___	Does the owning family provide education to the next generation on the rights and responsibilities of ownership?
37.	___	___	Are the family owners closely monitoring the business's strategy, culture, and board of directors?
38.	___	___	Do non-employed family owners avoid meddling in management's operating responsibilities?
39.	___	___	Does the owning family have respect for managers and the challenges of managing?
40.	___	___	Is the owning family active in educational programs on such topics as interpersonal relations and understanding business?
41.	___	___	Is the owning family committed to helping all family members in their professional development, regardless of their interests?
42.	___	___	Does the family have a policy on how best to address family members who may be in financial need?
43.	___	___	Are there many different roles family owners can play in the family council or other family interests?
44.	___	___	Does the family have a philanthropic activity?
45.	___	___	Are family branch politics and representation avoided in favor of everyone seeing themselves as members of one extended family?
46.	___	___	Has the owning family articulated a mission for the family?
47.	___	___	Has the family articulated how its values are important to the family's business.
48.	___	___	Does the owning family feel that the family business has a social purpose?
49.	___	___	Does the owning family believe in having a family-continuity planning process?
50.	___	___	Is the family active in promoting and supporting the concept of family business in its community?

Notes

1 The Ultimate Management Challenge

1 Ward, *Keeping the Family Business Healthy*, p. 2.
2 Ibid.
3 "For Your Children's Children's Children," p. 6.

2 The Five Insights and The Four P's

1 Barboza, "At Johnson Wax," *The New York Times*, August 22, 1999.
2 Tagiuri and Davis, "Bivalent Attributes," p. 200.
3 Myer, *Living the Dream*, p. 36.
4 Ibid., p. 114.
5 Ibid., p. 163.
6 Ibid., pp. 166–67.
7 Arthur Andersen/MassMutual American Family Business Surveys of 1997 and 2000.
8 Myer, *Living the Dream*, pp. 192–95.
9 Hochman, "Family Business," p. 21.
10 "Once Again, A Ford Sits Atop Ford," p. A5.
11 "Ford Family Takes the Helm," p. C9.
12 Crosbie, *Don't Leave It to the Children*, pp. 156–57.
13 Tifft and Jones, *The Trust*, pp. 628–29.
14 Myer, *Living the Dream*, pp. 244–47.
15 Ibid., p. 258.
16 Ibid., pp. 266–70.
17 Ibid, pp. 274–75.
18 Ibid., p. 106.
19 Hurstak and Raiser, "Salvatore Ferragamo, SpA," p. 9.
20 Tifft and Jones, *The Trust*, p. 25.
21 Tifft and Jones, *The Patriarch*, p. 43.
22 Ibid., p. 62.
23 Ibid., pp. 71–74.
24 Ibid., pp. 119–24.
25 Ibid., p. 478.
26 Tifft and Jones, *The Trust*, p. 10.
27 Ibid., pp. 15–18.
28 Ibid., p. 19.

3 A Vision for the Future

1 Chapter 3 is adapted from the paper, "Family Vision, Ownership Structure and Strategy Formulation for Family Firms," by John L. Ward.
2 Totten and Bibko, "Gekkeikan," pp. 34–35.
3 Ibid., p. 38.
4 Ward, "How Family Affects Strategy," *Families in Business*, November 2002, pp. 17–20.
5 Tifft and Jones, *The Trust*, p. 87.
6 Ibid., pp. 159 and 165–66.
7 Ibid., pp. 165–66.
8 Dryfoos, *Iphigene*, p. 174.
9 Tifft and Jones, *The Patriarch*, p. 150.

4 Stage I: The Owner-Managed Business

1 Longaberger, *Longaberger*, pp. xiii–xiv.
2 Ibid., p. xii.
3 Al. Neyer, Inc. 1998 Annual Report, n. pag.
4 Kanoo, *The House of Kanoo*, p. 285.
5 Smorgon, *Living the Dream*, pp. 163–64.
6 Ibid., p. 120.
7 Gordon, Epilogue, *MacMillan: The American Grain Family*, pp. 306–08.
8 Crosbie, *Don't Leave It to the Children*, pp. 154–56 and 165.
9 Aronoff and Ward, *More Than Family: Non-Family Executives in the Family Business*, p. 44.
10 Crosbie, *Don't Leave It to the Children*, p. 161.
11 Tifft and Jones, *The Trust*, p. 63.
12 Ibid., p. 59.
13 Ibid., pp. 81–82.
14 Ibid., pp. 90–91.
15 Ibid., p. 50.
16 Ibid., p. 64.
17 Ibid., p. 165.
18 Ibid., p. 185.
19 Ibid., p. 199.
20 Ibid., pp. 302 and 315.
21 Ibid., pp. 376–77.
22 Tifft and Jones, *The Patriarch*, pp. 47–48.
23 Ibid., p. 52.
24 Ibid., p. 111.
25 Ibid., p. 126.
26 Ibid., p. 145.
27 Ibid., pp. 142–46.
28 Ibid., p. 154.
29 Ibid., pp., 179–80 and 198.
30 Ibid., p. 162.
31 Ibid., p. 257.
32 Tifft and Jones, *The Trust*, p. 60.
33 Ibid., p. 154.

34　Tifft and Jones, *The Patriarch*, p. 80.
35　Ibid., p. 480.

5　Stage II: The Sibling Partnership

 1　Gibson, "A Case for the Family-Owned Conglomerate," pp. 133–34.
 2　Ibid., p. 135.
 3　Sonepar, January 17, 2003, <http://www.sonepar.com/front?id=sonepar/group&languageId=us>.
 4　Ferrand and de Villers, *Sonepar or the Quintessence of Things*, p. 192.
 5　Ibid., pp. 48–49.
 6　Kanoo, *The House of Kanoo*, p. 283.
 7　Ibid., pp. 284 and 77.
 8　Freudenberg Group, October 21, 2002, <http://www.freudenberg.com/company/portrait.htm>.
 9　Freudenberg Group, October 21, 2002, <http://www.freudenberg.com/tannerinfo/tanner.htm>.
10　Freudenberg Group, October 21, 2002, <http://www.freudenberg.com/history/sozial.htm>.
11　Kanoo, *The House of Kanoo*, p. 259.
12　Ibid., p. 260.
13　Ibid., p. 261.
14　Crosbie, *Don't Leave It to the Children*, p. 154.
15　Ibid., p. 159.
16　Gibbon and Hadekel, *Steinberg: The Breakup of a Family Empire*, pp. 109–11.
17　Ibid., p. 110.
18　Ibid., p. 112.
19　Ibid., pp. 158–60.
20　Ibid., pp. 121 and 170–71.
21　Gibson, "A Case for the Family-Owned Conglomerate," p. 136.
22　Zsolnay and Ward, "Succession and Continuity for Johnson Family Enterprises," Part A, p. 3.
23　Ibid., pp. 5 and 13.
24　Blondel and Van der Heyden, "Multi-generational French Family Firms," *Families in Business*, Volume 1, Issue 3 (April 2002), pp. 47–50.
25　"Wendel Investissement," February 11, 2003, <http://www.hoovers.com/co/capsule/2/0,2163,92042,00.html>.
26　Kenyon-Rouvinez, Adler, Corbetta, and Cuneo, *Sharing Wisdom, Building Values*, p. 13.
27　Tifft and Jones, *The Trust*, p. 184.
28　Brenner, *House of Dreams*, p. 363.
29　Tifft and Jones, *The Patriarch*, pp. 157 and 202–05.
30　Ibid., pp. 202–03.
31　Ibid., p. 229.
32　Ibid., pp. 241–48.
33　Ibid., pp. 251–55.
34　Ibid., p. 287.
35　Ibid., pp. 294–95.
36　Ibid., p. 289.
37　Ibid., p. 335.
38　Ibid., p. 337.
39　Ibid., p. 340.

40 Ibid., p. 339.
41 Ibid., p. 366.
42 Ibid., pp. 389–90.
43 Ibid., pp. 474–75.
44 Tifft and Jones, *The Trust*, p. 194.
45 Ibid., p. 758.
46 Ibid., p. 523.
47 Ibid., p. 535.
48 Ibid., pp. 480–81.
49 Ibid., p. 453.
50 Ibid., p. 474.
51 Ibid., p. xvi.
52 Ibid., p. 585.
53 Ibid.
54 Ibid., pp. 629–33.

6   Stage III: The Cousin Collaboration

1 Kenyon-Rouvinez, Adler, Corbetta, and Cuneo, *Sharing Wisdom, Building Values*, p. 25.
2 Kanoo, *The House of Kanoo*, p. 271.
3 Ibid., p. 272.
4 Ibid., p. 267.
5 Johnson, "Why We'll Never Go Public," p. 17.
6 Schwass, "Henkel Group," p. 6.
7 Kenyon-Rouvinez, *Sharing Wisdom, Building Values*, pp. 9–10.
8 Pellegrin, "Family Business Best Practices Learned from the LEGO Group," p. 1.
9 "Marriotts Oversee Closing of Last Hot Shoppes Restaurant," December 2, 1999, <http:// foxmarketwire.com/wires/1201/fap120148.sml>.
10 Marriott International, February 13, 2001, <http://www.marriott.com/milestone.asp>.
11 Marriott Foundation, February 12, 2003, <http://www.marriottfoundation.org/facts.htm>.
12 Schwass, "Henkel Group," pp 4–5.
13 Schwass and Wagen, "Hermès," p. 1.
14 Crosbie, *Don't Leave It to the Children*, pp. 159–60.
15 Schwass and Wagen, "Hermès," p. 1.
16 Ward, "Murugappa Group," pp. 29–31.
17 Crosbie, *Don't Leave It to the Children*, pp. 162–63.
18 Schwass, "Henkel Group," p. 4.
19 Kanoo, *The House of Kanoo*, p. 280.
20 Zsolnay and Ward, "Succession and Continuity for Johnson Family Enterprises," Part B, pp. 6–7.
21 Ward, "Murugappa Group," p. 28.
22 Levi Strauss & Co., January 30, 2003, <http://levistrauss.com/responsibility/foundation/>.
23 Evelyn & Walter Haas, Jr. Fund, January 30, 2003, <http://www.haasjr.org/who_whj.htm>.
24 Gibbon and Hadekel, *Steinberg: The Breakup of a Family Empire*, pp. 268–72.
25 Forden, *The House of Gucci*, p. 28.
26 Ibid., p. 30.
27 Ibid., pp. 69–70.
28 Ibid., p. 77.

29 Ibid., pp. 107–10.
30 Ibid., pp. 124–25.
31 Schwass, "The Zegna Group," p. 28.
32 Ibid., p. 31.
33 Wagen, "Corporación Puig," p. 7.
34 Kanoo, *The House of Kanoo*, p. 210.
35 Gibson, "A Case for the Family-Owned Conglomerate," pp. 128–29.
36 Schwass, "Henkel Group," p. 5.
37 Tifft and Jones, *The Trust*, pp. 630–31.
38 Ibid., p. 639.
39 Ibid., pp. 635–37.
40 Ibid., p. 722.
41 Ibid.
42 Ibid., p. 723.
43 Ibid., p. 758.
44 Ibid., p. 759.
45 Ibid., pp. 763–64.
46 Ibid., p. 585.

7   Taking the Longest View

1   Schwass, "Henkel Group," p. 6.
2   Tifft and Jones, *The Trust*, p. 100.
3   Kanoo, *The House of Kanoo*, p. 274.
4   Ferrand and de Villers, *The Essence of Things*, pp. 27–28.
5   Forden, *The House of Gucci*, p. 144.
6   Tifft and Jones, *The Patriarch*, p. 346.
7   Kanoo, *The House of Kanoo*, pp. 285–86; e-mail correspondence from Khalid Kanoo to the author, January 8, 2003.
8   Kanoo, *The House of Kanoo*, p. 153.
9   Ibid., p. 270.
10 Ibid.
11 Tifft and Jones, *The Patriarch*, p. 362.
12 Ibid., p. 312.
13 Schwass and Wagen, "Hermès," n. pag.
14 Wagen, "Corporación Puig," p. 7.
15 Tifft and Jones, *The Trust*, p. 154.
16 Myer, *Living the Dream*, pp. 275–78.
17 Ibid., p. 293.
18 Ibid., p. 285.
19 Ibid., p. 286.
20 Ibid., p. 289.

Bibliography

Al. Neyer, Inc. 1998 Annual Report. Cincinnati, 1999.

Aronoff, Craig E. and John L. Ward. *More than Family: Non-Family Executives in the Family Business*. Family Business Leadership Ser. 13. Marietta, Georgia: Business Owner Resources, 2000.

Barboza, David. "At Johnson Wax, A Family Hands Down its Heirloom." *New York Times*, August 22, 1999.

Blondel, Christine and Ludo Van der Heyden. "Multi-generational French Family Firms." *Families in Business*, Volume 1, Issue 3 (April 2002), pp. 47–50.

Brenner, Marie. *House of Dreams: The Bingham Family of Louisville*. New York: Random House, 1988.

Carlock, Randel and John L. Ward, *Strategic Planning for the Family Business*, London: Palgrave, 2001.

Collier, Peter and David Horowitz. *The Rockefellers: An American Dynasty*. New York: Holt, Rinehart and Winston, 1976.

Crosbie, Alan. *Don't Leave It to the Children: Starting, Building and Sustaining a Family Business*. Dublin: Marino Books, 2000.

Dryfoos, Susan W. *Iphigene: Memoirs of Iphigene Ochs Sulzberger of* The New York Times *Family*. New York: Dodd, Mead & Company, 1981.

Evelyn Hass and Walter Haas, Jr. Fund. Who We Are. January 30, 2003. <http://www.haasjr.org/who_whj.htm>.

Ferrand, Franck and Thibaut de Villers. *Sonepar or the Quintessence of Things*. Trans. Elizabeth Gruninger. [n.p.] Sonepar, 1998.

"For Your Children's Children's Children." *Family Business Advisor*, Volume 7, Issue 5 (May 1998), pp. 1, 6–7.

Forden, Sara Gay. *The House of Gucci: A Sensational Story of Murder, Madness, Glamour, and Greed*. New York: William Morrow, 2000.

Freudenberg Group. Portrait. October 21, 2002. <http://www.freudenberg.com/company/portrait.htm>.

Freudenberg Group. Social Responsibility. October 21, 2002. <http://www.freudenberg.com/history/sozial.htm>.

Freudenberg Group. Youth Programme TANNER. October 21, 2002. <http://www.freudenberg.com/tannerinfo/tanner.htm>.

Gibbon, Ann and Peter Hadekel. *Steinberg: The Breakup of a Family Empire*. Toronto: MacMillan of Canada, 1990.

Gibson, Ken. "A Case for the Family-Owned Conglomerate." *McKinsey Quarterly*, Issue 4 (2002).

Gordon, John Steele. Epilogue. *MacMillan: The American Grain Family*. By W. Duncan MacMillan with Patricia Condon Johnston. Afton, Minnesota: Afton Historical Society Press, 1998.

Hakim, Danny. "Ford Family Takes the Helm." *New York Times*, October 31, pp. C1, C9.

Hochman, Gloria. "Family Business on the Couch." *Inquirer Magazine* [Philadelphia], December 21, 2001, pp. 19–22.

Hurstak, Johanna M. and Jennifer Raiser. "Salvatore Ferragamo, SpA." Boston: Harvard Business School, 1991, rev. 1993.

Johnson, Samuel C. "Why We'll Never Go Public." *Family Business*, Volume 1, Issue 4 (May 1990), pp. 16–21.

Kanoo, Khalid M. *The House of Kanoo: A Century of an Arabian Family Business*. London: The London Centre of Arab Studies, 1997.

——. E-mail correspondence to the author. January 8, 2003.

Kenyon-Rouvinez, Denise H., Gordon Adler, Guido Corbetta and Gianfilippo Cuneo. *Sharing Wisdom, Building Values: Letters from Family Business Owners to Their Successors*. Marietta, Georgia: Family Enterprise Publishers, 2002.

Levi Strauss & Co. Social Responsibility/Levi Strauss Foundation. January 30, 2003. <http:// levistrauss.com/responsibility/foundation/>.

Longaberger, Dave. *Longaberger: An American Success Story*. New York: HarperBusiness, 2001.

Marriott Foundation. Just the Facts. February 12, 2003. <http://www.marriottfoundation.org/facts.htm>.

Marriott International. Marriott History. February 13, 2001. February 12, 2003. http://www.marriott.com/milestone.asp>.

"Marriotts Oversee Closing of Last Hot Shoppes Restaurant." Fox Market Wire. December 2, 1999. January 16, 2000. <http://foxmarketwire.com/wires/120/f_ap_1201_48.sml>.

Myer, Rod. *Living the Dream: The Story of Victor Smorgon*. Sydney: New Holland Publishers, 2000.

"Once Again, A Ford Sits Atop Ford." *Investor's Business Daily*, October 31, 2001, p. A5.

Pellegrin, Jonathan. "Family Business Best Practices Learned from the LEGO Group." Lausanne: IMD, 1996, Switzerland.

Rockefeller, David. *Memoirs*. New York: Random House, 2002.

Sonepar. Sonepar Overview. January 17, 2003. <http:// www.sonepar.com/front?id=sonepar/group&languageId=us>.

Schwass, Joachim. "Henkel Group." Lausanne, Switzerland: IMD, 1999.

——. "The Zegna Group." *Families in Business*, Issue 1 (Autumn 2001), pp. 27–31.

Schwass, Joachim and Monica Wagen. "Hermès: Winner of the 1997 IMD Distinguished Family Business Award." Lausanne, Switzerland: IMD, 1997.

Tagiuri, Renato and John Davis. "Bivalent Attributes of the Family Firm." Working Paper, Harvard Business School, Cambridge, MA. Reprinted *Family Business Review*, Volume 9, Issue 2 (Summer 1996), pp. 199–208.

Tifft, Susan E. and Alex S. Jones. *The Patriarch: The Rise and Fall of the Bingham Dynasty*. New York: Summit Books, 1991.

——. *The Trust: The Private and Powerful Family Behind* The New York Times. Boston: Little, Brown and Co., 1999.

Totten, Sonia and Suzy Bibko. "Gekkeikan." *Families in Business*, Volume 1, Issue 4 (June 2002), pp. 34–38.

Wagen, Monica. "Corporación Puig." F.B.N. Newsletter, No. 22 (December 1998), pp. 5–9.

Waldie, Paul and Kate Jennison. *A House Divided: The Untold Story of the McCain Family*. Toronto: Viking, 1996.

Ward, John L. *Keeping the Family Business Healthy: How to Plan for Continuing Growth, Profitability, and Family Leadership*. San Francisco: Jossey-Bass, 1987.

——. "Family Vision, Ownership Structure and Strategy Formulation for Family Firms." Presented to Academy of Management, August 1996.

——. "How Family Affects Strategy." *Families in Business*, November 2002, pp. 17–20.

——. "Murugappa Group." *Families in Business*, Volume 1, Issue 2 (February 2002), pp. 26–31.

"Wendel Investissement." Hoover's Online. February 11, 2003, <http://www.hoovers.com/co/capsule/2/0,2163,92042,00.html>.

Zsolnay, Carol Adler and John L. Ward. "Succession and Continuity for Johnson Family Enterprises." Evanston: Kellogg School of Management, Northwestern University, 2002.

Index